D1596055

PRINCIPLES OF FREEDOM

KENNIKAT PRESS SCHOLARLY REPRINTS

Ralph Adams Brown, Senior Editor

Series In
IRISH HISTORY AND CULTURE
Under the General Editorial Supervision of
Gilbert A. Cahill
Professor of History, State University of New York

TERENCE MACSWINEY
(Late Lord Mayor of Cork)

PRINCIPLES OF FREEDOM

BY
TERENCE J. MacSWINEY
LATE LORD MAYOR OF CORK

KENNIKAT PRESS
Port Washington, N. Y./London

PRINCIPLES OF FREEDOM

First published in 1921
Reissued in 1970 by Kennikat Press
Library of Congress Catalog Card No: 73-102616
SBN 8046-0793-1

Manufactured by Taylor Publishing Company   Dallas, Texas

KENNIKAT SERIES IN IRISH HISTORY AND CULTURE

PREFACE

It was my intention to publish these articles in book form as soon as possible. I had them typed for the purpose. I had no time for revision save to insert in the typed copy words or lines omitted from the original printed matter. I also made an occasional verbal alteration in the original. One article, however, that on " Intellectual Freedom," though written in the series in the place in which it now stands, was not printed with them. It is now published for the first time.

Religion

I wish to make a note on the article under this heading to avoid a possible misconception amongst people outside Ireland. In Ireland there is no religious dissension, but there is religious sincerity. English politicians, to serve the end of

dividing Ireland, have worked on the religious feelings of the North, suggesting
the danger of Catholic ascendancy. There
is not now, and there never was, any such
danger, but our enemies, by raising the
cry, sowed discord in the North, with the
aim of destroying Irish unity. It should
be borne in mind that when the Republican Standard was first raised in the field
in Ireland, in the Rising of 1798, Catholics
and Protestants in the North were united
in the cause. Belfast was the first home
of Republicanism in Ireland. This is the
truth of the matter. The present-day
cleavage is an unnatural thing created by
Ireland's enemies to hold her in subjection and will disappear entirely with
political Freedom.

It has had, however, in our day, one
unhappy effect, only for a time for-
tunately, and this is disappearing. I refer
to the rise of Hibernianism. The English
ruling faction having, for their own political designs, corrupted the Orangemen
with power and flattery, enabled them to
establish an ascendancy not only over
Ulster, but indirectly by their vote over
the South. This becoming intolerable,

some sincere but misguided Catholics in the North joined the organisation known as THE ANCIENT ORDER OF HIBERNIANS. This was, in effect, a sort of Catholic Freemasonry to counter the Orange Freemasonry, but like Orangeism, it was a political and not a religious weapon.

Further, as a political weapon, it extended all through Ireland during the last years of the Irish Parliamentary Movement. In Cork, for example, it completely controlled the city life for some years, but the rapid rise of the Republican Movement brought about the equally rapid fall of Hibernianism. At the present moment it has as little influence in the public life of Cork as Sir Edward Carson himself. The great bulk of its one-time members have joined the Republican Movement. This demonstrates clearly that anything in the nature of a sectarian movement is essentially repugnant to the Irish people. As I have pointed out, the Hibernian Order, when created, became at once a political weapon, but Ireland has discarded that, and other such weapons, for those with which she is carving out the

destinies of the Republic. For a time,
however, Hibernianism created an unnatural atmosphere of sectarian rivalry in
Ireland. That has now happily passed
away. At the time, however, of the
writing of the article on Religion it was
at its height, and this fact coloured the
writing of the article. On re-reading it
and considering the publication of the
present work I was inclined to suppress
it, but decided that it ought to be included
because it bears directly on the evil of
materialism in religious bodies, which is
a matter of grave concern to every religious community in the world.

T. MacS.

CONTENTS

PRINCIPLES OF FREEDOM

CHAPTER I

THE BASIS OF FREEDOM

I

WHY should we fight for freedom? Is it not strange, that it has become necessary to ask and answer this question? We have fought our fight for centuries, and contending parties still continue the struggle, but the real significance of the struggle and its true motive force are hardly at all understood, and there is a curious but logical result. Men technically on the same side are separated by differences wide and deep, both of ideal and plan of action; while, conversely, men technically opposed have perhaps more in common than we realise in a sense deeper than we understand.

II

This is the question I would discuss. I find in practice everywhere in Ireland—it is worse out of Ireland—the doctrine, "The end justifies the means."

One party will denounce another for the use of discreditable tactics, but it will have no hesitation in using such itself if it can thereby snatch a discreditable victory. So, clear speaking is needed : a fight that is not clean-handed will make victory more disgraceful than any defeat. I make the point here because we stand for separation from the British Empire, and because I have heard it argued that we ought, if we could, make a foreign alliance to crush English power here, even if our foreign allies were engaged in crushing freedom elsewhere. When such a question can be proposed it should be answered, though the time is not ripe to test it. If Ireland were to win freedom by helping directly or indirectly to crush another people she would earn the execration she has herself poured out on tyranny for ages. I have come to see it is possible for Ireland to win her independence by base methods. It is imperative, therefore, that we should declare ourselves and know where we stand. And I stand by this principle : no physical victory can compensate for spiritual surrender. Whatever side denies that is not my side.

What, then, is the true basis to our claim to freedom? There are two points of view. The first we have when fresh from school, still in our teens, ready to tilt against everyone and everything, delighting in saying smart things—and able sometimes to say them—talking much and boldly of freedom, but satisfied if the thing sounds bravely. There is the later point of view. We are no longer boys; we have come to review the situation, and take a definite stand in life. We have had years of experience, keen struggles, not a little bitterness, and we are steadied. We feel a heart-beat for deeper things. It is no longer sufficient that they sound bravely; they must ring true. The schoolboy's dream is more of a Roman triumph —tramping armies, shouting multitudes, waving banners—all good enough in their way. But the dream of men is for something beyond all this show. If it were not, it could hardly claim a sacrifice.

III

A spiritual necessity makes the true significance of our claim to freedom : the material aspect is only a secondary consideration. A man facing life is gifted with certain powers of soul and body. It is of vital importance to himself and the community that he be given a full opportunity to develop his powers, and to fill his place worthily. In a free state he is in the natural environment for full self-development. In an enslaved state it is the reverse. When one country holds another in subjection that other suffers materially and morally. It suffers materially, being a prey for plunder. It suffers morally because of the corrupt influences the bigger nation sets at work to maintain its ascendancy. Because of this moral corruption national subjection should be resisted, as a state fostering vice; and as in the case of vice, when we understand it we have no option but to fight. With it we can make no terms. It is the duty of the rightful power to develop the best in its subjects : it is the practice of the usurping power to develop the basest. Our history affords many examples. When our rulers visit Ireland they bestow favours and titles on the supporters of their regime— but it is always seen that the greatest favours and highest titles are not for the honest adherent of their power—but for him who has betrayed the national cause that he entered public life to support. Observe the men who might be respected are passed over for him who ought to be despised. In the corrupt politician there was surely a better nature. A free state would have encouraged and developed it. The usurping state titled him for the use of his baser instincts. Such allurement must mean demoralisation. We are none of us angels, and under the best of circumstances find it hard to do worthy things; when all the temptation is to do unworthy things we are demoralised. Most of us, happily, will not give ourselves over to the evil influence, but we lose faith in the ideal. We are apathetic. We have powers and let them lie fallow. Our minds should be restless for noble and beautiful things; they are hopeless in a land everywhere confined and wasted. In the destruction

B

of spirit entailed lies the deeper significance of our claim to freedom.

IV

It is a spiritual appeal, then, that primarily moves us. We are urged to action by a beautiful ideal. The motive force must be likewise true and beautiful. It is love of country that inspires us; not hate of the enemy and desire for full satisfaction for the past. Pause awhile. We are all irritated now and then by some mawkish interpretation of our motive force that makes it seem a weakly thing, invoked to help us in evading difficulties instead of conquering them. Love in any genuine form is strong, vital and warm-blooded. Let it not be confused with any flabby substitute. Take a parallel case. Should we, because of the mawkishness of a "Princess Novelette," deride the beautiful dream that keeps ages wondering and joyous, that is occasionally caught up in the words of genius, as when Shelley sings: "I arise from dreams of thee"? When foolish people make a sacred thing seem silly, let us at least be sane. The man who cries out for the sacred thing but voices a universal need. To exist, the healthy mind must have beautiful things —the rapture of a song, the music of running water, the glory of the sunset and its dreams, and the deeper dreams of the dawn. It is nothing but love of country that rouses us to make our land full-blooded and beautiful where now she is pallid and wasted. This, too, has its deeper significance.

V

If we want full revenge for the past the best way to get it is to remain as we are. As we are, Ireland is a menace to England. We need not debate this—she herself admits it by her continued efforts to pacify us in her own stupid way. Would she not ignore us if it were quite safe so to do? On the other hand, if we succeed in our efforts to separate from her, the benefit to England will be second only to our own. This might strike us strangely, but 'tis true, not the less true because the English people could hardly understand or appreciate it now. The military defence of Ireland is almost farcical. A free

Ireland could make it a reality—could make it strong against invasion. This would secure England from attack on our side. No one is, I take it, so foolish as to suppose, being free, we would enter quarrels not our own. We should remain neutral. Our common sense would so dictate, our sense of right would so demand. The freedom of a nation carries with it the responsibility that it be no menace to the freedom of another nation. The freedom of all makes for the security of all. If there are tyrannies on earth one nation cannot set things right, but it is still bound so to order its own affairs as to be consistent with universal freedom and friendship. And, again, strange as it may seem, separation from England will alone make for final friendship with England. For no one is so foolish as to wish to be for ever at war with England. It is unthinkable. Now the most beautiful motive for freedom is vindicated. Our liberty stands to benefit the enemy instead of injuring him. If we want to injure him, we should remain as we are—a menace to him. The opportunity will come, but it would hardly make us happy. This but makes clear a need of the human race.

Freedom rightly considered is not a mere setting-up of a number of independent units. It makes for harmony among nations and good fellowship on earth.

VI

I have written carefully that no one may escape the conclusion. It is clear and exacting, but in the issue it is beautiful. We fight for freedom—not for the vanity of the world, not to have a fine conceit of ourselves, not to be as bad—or if we prefer to put it so, as big as our neighbours. The inspiration is drawn from a deeper element of our being. We stifle for self-development individually and as a nation. If we don't go forward we must go down. It is a matter of life and death; it is our soul's salvation. If the whole nation stand for it, we are happy; we shall be grandly victorious. If only a few are faithful found they must be the more steadfast for being but a few. They stand for an individual right that is inalienable. A majority has no right to annul it, and no power to destroy it. Tyrannies may persecute, slay, or banish those who defend it; the thing is indestructible. It does not need legions to protect it nor genius to proclaim it, though the poets have always glorified it, and the legions will ultimately acknowledge it. One man alone may vindicate it, and because that one man has never failed it has never died. Not, indeed, that Ireland has ever been reduced to a single loyal son. She never will be. We have not survived the centuries to be conquered now. But the profound significance of the struggle, of its deep spiritual appeal, of the imperative need for a motive force as lofty and beautiful, of the consciousness that worthy winning of freedom is a labour for human brotherhood; the significance of it all is seen in the obligation it imposes on everyone to be true, the majority notwithstanding. He is called to a grave charge who is called to resist the majority. But he will resist, knowing his victory will lead them to a dearer dream than they had ever known. He will fight for that ideal in obscurity, little heeded—in the open, misunderstood; in humble places, still undaunted; in high places, seizing every vantage point, never crushed, never silent, never despairing, cheering a few comrades with hope for the morrow.

And should these few sink in the struggle the greatness of the ideal is proven in the last hour; as they fall their country awakens to their dream, and he who inspired and sustained them is justified; justified against the whole race, he who once stood alone against them. In the hour he falls he is the saviour of his race.

CHAPTER II

I

WHEN we plead for separation from the British Empire as the only basis on which our country can have full development, and on which we can have final peace with England, we find in opponents a variety of attitudes, but one attitude invariably absent—a readiness to discuss the question fairly and refute it, if this can be done. One man will take it superficially and heatedly, assuming it to be, according to his party, a censure on Mr. Redmond or Mr. O'Brien. Another will take it superficially, but, as he thinks, philosophically, and will dismiss it with a smile. With the followers of Mr. Redmond or Mr. O'Brien we can hardly argue at

present, but we should not lose heart on
their account, for these men move
en masse. One day the consciousness of
the country will be electrified with a great
deed or a great sacrifice and the multitude
will break from lethargy or prejudice and
march with a shout for freedom in a true,
a brave, and a beautiful sense. We must
work and prepare for that hour. Then
there is our philosophical friend. I expect
him to hear my arguments. When I am
done, he may not agree with me on all
points; he may not agree with me on any
point; but if he come with me, I promise
him one thing : this question can no longer
be dismissed with a smile.

II

Our friend's attitude is explained in part
by our never having attempted to show
that a separatist policy is great and wise.
We have held it as a right, have fought
for it, have made sacrifices for it, and
vowed to have it at any cost; but we have
not found for it a definite place in a
philosophy of life. Superficial though he
be, our friend has indicated a need : we
must take the question philosophically—

but in the great and true sense. It is a
truism of philosophy and science that the
world is a harmonious whole, and that
with the increase of knowledge, laws can
be discovered to explain the order and the
unity of the universe. Accordingly, if
we are to justify our own position as
separatists, we must show that it will
harmonise, unify and develop our national life, that it will restore us to a
place among the nations, enable us to
fulfil a national destiny, a destiny which,
through all our struggles, we ever believe
is great, and waiting for us. That must be
accepted if we are to get at the truth of
the matter. A great doctrine that domi-
nates our lives, that lays down a rigid
course of action, that involves self-denial,
hard struggles, endurance for years, and
possibly death before the goal is reached—
any such doctrine must be capable of
having its truth demonstrated by the dis-
covery of principles that govern and
justify it. Otherwise we cannot yield it
our allegiance. Let us to the examination,
then; we shall find it soul-stirring and
inspiring. We must be prepared, however, to abandon many deeply-rooted
prejudices; if we are unwilling, we must

abandon the truth. But we will find courage in moving forward, and will triumph in the end, by keeping in mind at all times that the end of freedom is to realise the salvation and happiness of all peoples, to make the world, and not any selfish corner of it, a more beautiful dwelling-place for men.

Treated in this light, the question becomes for all earnest men great and arresting. Our friend, who may have smiled, will discuss it readily now. Yet he may not be convinced; he may point his finger over the wasted land and contrast its weakness with its opponents' strength, and conclude : " Your philosophy is beautiful, but only a dream." He is at least impressed; that is a point gained; and we may induce him to come further and further till he adopts the great principle we defend.

III

His difficulty now is the common error that a man's work for his country should be based on the assumption that it should bear full effect in his own time. This is most certainly false; for a man's life is counted by years, a nation's by centuries, and as work for the nation should be directed to bringing her to full maturity in the coming time, a man must be prepared to labour for an end that may be realised only in another generation. Consider how he disposes his plans for his individual life. His boyhood and youth are directed that his manhood and prime may be the golden age of life, full-blooded and strong-minded, with clear vision and great purpose and high hope, all justified by some definite achievement. A man's prime is great as his earlier years have been well directed and concentrated. In the early years the ground is prepared and the seed sown for the splendid period of full development. So it is with the nation : we must prepare the ground and sow the seed for the rich ripeness of maturity; and bearing in mind that the maturity of the nation will come, not in one generation but after many generations, we must be prepared to work in the knowledge that we prepare for a future that only other generations will enjoy. It does not mean that we shall work in loneliness, cheered by no vision of the Promised Land; we may even reach the Promised Land in our time, though we cannot explore all its great wonders : that will be the delight of ages. But some will never survive to celebrate the great victory that will establish our independence; yet they shall not go without reward; for to them will come a vision of soul of the future triumph, an exaltation of soul in the consciousness of labouring for that future, an exultation of soul in the knowledge that once its purpose is grasped, no tyranny can destroy it, that the destiny of our country is assured, and her dominion will endure for ever. Let any argument be raised against one such pioneer—he knows this in his heart, and it makes him indomitable, and it is he who is proven to be wise in the end. He judges the past clearly, and through the crust of things he discerns the truth in his own time, and puts his work in true relation to the great experience of life, and he is justified; for ultimately his work opens out, matures, and bears fruit a hundredfold. It may not be in a day, but when his hand falls dead, his glory becomes quickly manifest. He has lived a beautiful life, and has left a beautiful field; he has sacrificed the hour to give service for all time; he has entered the company of the great, and with them he will be remembered for ever. He is the practical man in the true sense. But there is the other self-styled practical man, who thinks all this proceeding foolish, and cries out for the expedient of the hour. Has he ever realised the promise of his proposals? No, he is the most inefficient person who has ever walked the earth. But for a saving consideration let him go contemplate the wasted efforts of the opportunist in every generation, and the broken projects scattered through the desert-places of history.

IV

Still one will look out on the grim things of the hour, and hypnotised by the hour will cry : "See the strength of the British Empire, see our wasted state; your hope is vain." Let him consider this clear truth : peoples endure; empires perish. Where are now the empires of antiquity? And the empires of to-day have the seed of dissolution in them. But the peoples that saw the old empires rise and hold sway are represented now in their pos-terity; the tyrannies they knew are dead and done with. The peoples endured; the empires perished; and the nations of the earth of this day will survive in posterity when the empires that now contend for mastery are gathered into the dust, with all dead, bad things. We shall endure; and the measure of our faith will be the measure of our achievement and of the greatness of our future place.

v

Is it not the dream of earnest men of all parties to have an end to our long war, a peace final and honourable, wherein the soul of the country can rest, revive and express itself; wherein poetry, music and art will pour out in uninterrupted joy, the joy of deliverance, flashing in splendour and superabundant in volume, evidence of long suppression? This is the dream of us all. But who can hope for this final peace while any part of our independence is denied? For, while we are connected in any shape with the British Empire the connection implies some dependence; this cannot be gainsaid; and who is so foolish as to expect that there will be no collision with the British Parliament, while there is this connection implying dependence on the British Empire? If such a one exists he goes against all experience and all history. On either side of the connection will be two interests—the English interest and the Irish interest, and they will be always at variance. Consider how parties within a single state are at variance, Conservatives and Radicals, in any country in Europe. The proposals of one are always insidious, dangerous or reactionary, as the case may be, in the eyes of the other; and in no case will the parties agree; they will at times even charge each other with treachery; there is never peace. It is the rule of party war. Who, then, can hope for peace where into the strife is imported a race difference, where the division is not of party but of people? That is in truth the vain hope. And be it borne in mind the race difference is not due to our predominating Gaelic stock, but to the separate countries and to distinct households in the human race. If we were all of English extraction the difference would still exist. There is the historic case of the American States; it is easy to understand. When a man's children come of age, they set up establishments for themselves, and live independently; they are always bound by affection to the parent-home; but if the father try to interfere in the house of a son, and govern it in any detail, there will be strife. It is hardly necessary to labour the point. If all the people in this country were of English extraction and England were to claim on that account that there should be a connection with her, and that it should dominate the people here, there would be strife; and it could have but one end—separation. We would, of whatever extraction, have lived in natural neighbourliness with England, but she chose to trap and harass us, and it will take long generations of goodwill to wipe out some memories. Again, and yet again, let there be no confusion of thought as to this final peace; it will never come while there is any formal link of dependence. The spirit of our manhood will always flame up to resent and resist that link. Separation and equality may restore ties of friendship; nothing else can : for individual development and general goodwill is the lesson of human life. We can be good neighbours, but most dangerous enemies, and in the coming time our hereditary foe

c

cannot afford to have us on her flank.
The present is promising; the future is
developing for us : we shall reach the goal.
Let us see to it that we shall be found
worthy.

VI

That we be found worthy; let this be
borne in mind. For it is true that here
only is our great danger. If with our freedom to win, our country to open up, our
future to develop, we learn no lesson from
the mistakes of nations and live no better
life than the great Powers, we shall have
missed a golden opportunity, and shall be
one of the failures of history. So far,
on superficial judgment, we have been
accounted a failure; though the simple
maintenance of our fight for centuries has
been in itself a splendid triumph. But
then only would we have failed in the
great sense, when we had got our field and
wasted it, as the nations around us waste
theirs to-day. We led Europe once; let us
lead again with a beautiful realisation of freedom; and let us beware of the
delusion that is abroad, that we seek
nothing more than to be free of restraint,

as England, France and Germany are to-day; let us beware of the delusion that if we can scramble through anyhow to freedom we can then begin to live worthily, but that in the interval we cannot be too particular. That is the grim shadow that darkens our path, that falls between us and a beautiful human life, and may drive us to that tiger-like existence that makes havoc through the world to-day. Let us beware. I do not say we must settle now all disputes, such as capital, labour, and others, but that everyone should realise a duty to be high-minded and honourable in action; to regard his fellow not as a man to be circumvented, but as a brother to be sympathised with and uplifted. Neither kingdom, republic, nor commune can re-generate us; it is in the beautiful mind and a great ideal we shall find the charter of our freedom; and this is the philosophy that it is most essential to preach. We must not ignore it now, for how we work to-day will decide how we shall live to-morrow; and if we are not scrupulous in our struggle, we shall not be pure in our future state. I know there are many who are not indifferent to high-minded action, but who live in dread of an exacting code of life, fearing it will harass our movements and make success impossible. Let us correct this mistake with the reflection that the time is shaping for us. The power of our country is strengthening; the grip of the enemy is slackening; every extension of local government is a step nearer to independent government; the people are not satisfied with an instalment; their capacity for further power is developed, and they are equipped with weapons to win it. Even in our time have we made great advance. Let one fact alone make this evident. Less than twenty years ago the Irish language was despised; to-day the movement to restore it is strong enough to have it made compulsory in the National University. Can anyone doubt from this sign of the times alone that the hour points to freedom, and we are on the road to victory? That we shall win our freedom I have no doubt; that we shall use it well I am not so certain, for see how sadly misused it is abroad through the world to-day. That should be our final consideration, and we should make this a resolution—our future history shall be more glorious than that of any contemporary state. We shall look for prosperity, no doubt, but let our enthusiasm be for beautiful living; we shall build up our strength, yet not for conquest, but as a pledge of brotherhood and a defence for the weaker ones of the earth; we shall take pride in our institutions, not only as guaranteeing the stability of the state, but as securing the happiness of the citizens, and we shall lead Europe again as we led it of old. We shall rouse the world from a wicked dream of material greed, of tyrannical power, of corrupt and callous politics to the wonder of a regenerated spirit, a new and beautiful dream; and we shall establish our state in a true freedom that will endure for ever.

CHAPTER III

I

ONE of the great difficulties in discussing any question of importance in Ireland is that words have been twisted from their original and true significance, and if we are to have any effective discussion, we must first make clear the meaning of our terms. Love of country is quoted to tolerate every insidious error of weakness, but if it has any meaning it should make men strong-souled and resolute in every crisis. Men working for the extension of Local Government toast "Ireland a Nation," and extol Home Rule as independence; but while there is any restraint on us by a neighbouring Power, acknowledged superior, there is dependence to that extent. Straightway, those who fight for independence shift their ground and plead for absolute independence, but there is no such thing as qualified independence; and when we abandon the simple name to men of half-measures, we prejudice our cause and confuse the issue. Then there is the irreconcilable—how is he regarded in the common cry? Always an impossible, wild, foolish person, and we frequently resent the name and try to explain his reasonableness instead of exulting in his strength, for the true irreconcilable is the simple lover of the truth. Among men fighting for freedom some start up in their plea for liberty, pointing to the prosperity of England, France, and Germany, and when we debate the means by which they won their power, we find our friends draw no distinction between true freedom and licentious living; but it would be better to be crushed under the wheels of great Powers than to prosper by their example. And so, through every discussion we must make clear the meaning of our terms. There is one I would treat particularly now. Of all the terms glibly flung about in every debate not one has been so confused as Moral Force.

II

Since the time of O'Connell the cry
Moral Force has been used persistently to
cover up the weakness of every politician
who was afraid or unwilling to fight for
the whole rights of his country, and confusion has been the consequence. I am not
going here to raise old debates over O'Connell's memory, who, when all is said, was
a great man and a patriot. Let those of us
who read with burning eyes of the shame-
less fiasco of Clontarf recall for full
judgment the O'Connell of earlier years,
when his unwearied heart was fighting
the uphill fight of the pioneer. But a great
need now is to challenge his later influence, which is overshadowing us to our
undoing. For we find men of this time
who lack moral courage fighting in the
name of moral force, while those who are
pre-eminent as men of moral fibre are dismissed with a smile—physical-force men.
To make clear the confusion we need only
to distinguish moral force from moral
weakness. There is the distinction. Call
it what we will, moral courage, moral
strength, moral force; we all recognise

that great virtue of mind and heart that keeps a man unconquerable above every power of brute strength. I call it moral force, which is a good name, and I make the definition : a man of moral force is he who, seeing a thing to be right and essential and claiming his allegiance, stands for it as for the truth, unheeding any consequence. It is not that he is a wild person, utterly reckless of all mad possibilities, filled with a madder hope, and indifferent to any havoc that may ensue. No, but it is a first principle of his, that a true thing is a good thing, and from a good thing rightly pursued can follow no bad consequence. And he faces every possible development with conscience at rest—it may be with trepidation for his own courage in some great ordeal, but for the nobility of the cause and the beauty of the result that must ensue, always with serene faith. And soon the trepidation for himself passes, for a great cause always makes great men, and many who set out in hesitation die heroes. This it is that explains the strange and wonderful buoyancy of men, standing for great ideals, so little understood of others of weaker mould. The soldier of freedom knows he is forward in the battle of Truth, he knows his victory will make for a world beautiful, that if he must inflict or endure pain, it is for the regeneration of those who suffer, the emancipation of those in chains, the exaltation of those who die, and the security and happiness of generations yet unborn. For the strength that will support a man through every phase of this struggle a strong and courageous mind is the primary need—in a word, Moral Force. A man who will be brave only if tramping with a legion will fail in courage if called to stand in the breach alone. And it must be clear to all that till Ireland can again summon her banded armies there will be abundant need for men who will stand the single test. 'Tis the bravest test, the noblest test, and 'tis the test that offers the surest and greatest victory. For one armed man cannot resist a multitude, nor one army conquer countless legions; but not all the armies of all the Empires of earth can crush the spirit of one true man. And that one man will prevail.

III

But so much have we felt the need of
resisting every slavish tendency that
found refuge under the name of Moral
Force, that those of us who would vindicate our manhood cried wildly out again
for the physical test; and we cried it long
and repeatedly the more we smarted under the meanness of retrograde times. But
the time is again inspiring, and the air
must now be cleared. We have set up for
the final test of the man of unconquerable
spirit that test which is the first and last
argument of tyranny—recourse to brute
strength. We have surrounded with fic-
titious glory the carnage of the battlefields;
we have shouted of wading through our
enemies' blood, as if bloody fields were
beautiful; we have been contemptuous of
peace, as if every war were exhilarating;
but, "War is hell," said a famous general
in the field. This, of course, is exaggeration, but there is a grim element of truth
in the warning that must be kept in mind
at all times. If one among us still would
resent being asked to forego what he
thinks a rightful need of vengeance, let

him look into himself. Let him consider
his feelings on the death of some notorious
traitor or criminal; not satisfaction, but
awe, is the uppermost feeling in his heart.
Death sobers us all. But away from death
this may be unconvincing; and one may
still shout of the glory of floating the ship
of freedom in the blood of the enemy. I
give him pause. He may still correct his
philosophy in view of the horror of a street
accident or the brutality of a prize-fight.

IV

But war must be faced and blood must
be shed, not gleefully, but as a terrible
necessity, because there are moral horrors
worse than any physical horror, because
freedom is indispensable for a soul erect,
and freedom must be had at any cost of
suffering; the soul is greater than the body.
This is the justification of war. If hesi-
tating to undertake it means the overthrow
of liberty possessed, or the lying passive in
slavery already accomplished, then it is the
duty of every man to fight if he is standing,
or revolt if he is down. And he must make
no peace till freedom is assured, for the
moral plague that eats up a people whose

independence is lost is more calamitous than any physical rending of limb from limb. The body is a passing phase; the spirit is immortal; and the degradation of that immortal part of man is the great tragedy of life. Consider all the mean things and debasing tendencies that wither up a people in a state of slavery. There are the bribes of those in power to maintain their ascendancy, the barter of every principle by time-servers; the corruption of public life and the apathy of private life; the hard struggle of those of high ideals, the conflict with all ignoble practices, the wearing down of patience, and in the end the quiet abandoning of the flag once bravely flourished; then the increased numbers of the apathetic and the general gloom, depression, and despair—everywhere a land decaying. Viciousness, meanness, cowardice, intolerance, every bad thing arises like a weed in the night and blights the land where freedom is dead; and the aspect of that land and the soul of that people become spectacles of disgust, revolting and terrible, terrible for the high things degraded and the great destinies imperilled. It would be less terrible if an earthquake split the land in two, and sank it into the

ocean. To avert the moral plague of
slavery men fly to arms, notwithstanding
the physical consequence, and those who
set more count by the physical consequences cannot by that avert them, for the
moral disease is followed by physical
wreck—if delayed still inevitable. So,
physical force is justified, not *per se*, but
as an expression of moral force; where it
is unsupported by the higher principle it
is evil incarnate. The true antithesis is
not between moral force and physical
force, but between moral force and moral
weakness. That is the fundamental distinction being ignored on all sides. When
the time demands and the occasion offers,
it is imperative to have recourse to arms,
but in that terrible crisis we must preserve
our balance. If we leap forward for our
enemies' blood, glorifying brute force, we
set up the standard of the tyrant and heap
up infamy for ourselves; on the other
hand, if we hesitate to take the stern action
demanded, we fail in strength of soul, and
let slip the dogs of war to every extreme of
weakness and wildness, to create depravity
and horror that will ultimately destroy us.
A true soldier of freedom will not hesitate
to strike vigorously and strike home,

knowing that on his resolution will depend
the restoration and defence of liberty. But
he will always remember that restraint is
the great attribute that separates man from
beast, that retaliation is the vicious resource of the tyrant and the slave; that
magnanimity is the splendour of manhood; and he will remember that he strikes
not at his enemy's life, but at his misdeed,
that in destroying the misdeed, he makes
not only for his own freedom, but even for
his enemy's regeneration. This may be for
most of us perhaps too great a dream. But
for him who reads into the heart of the
question and for the true shaping of his
course it will stand; he will never forget,
even in the thickest fight, that the enemy
of to-day and yesterday may be the
genuine comrade of to-morrow.

v

If it is imperative that we should fix
unalterably our guiding principles before
we are plunged unprepared into the fight,
it is even more urgent we should clear the
mind to the truth now, for we have fallen
into the dangerous habit of deferring important questions on the plea that the time

is not ripe. In a word, we lack moral strength; and so, that virtue that is to safeguard us in time of war is the great virtue that will redeem us in time of servility. It need not be further laboured that in a state enslaved every mean thing flourishes. The admission of it makes clear that in such a state it is more important that every evil be resisted. In a normal condition of liberty many temporary evils may arise; yet they are not dangerous—in the glow of a people's freedom they waste and die as disease dies in the sunlight. But where independence is suppressed and a people degenerate, a little evil is in an atmosphere to grow, and it grows and expands; and evils multiply and destroy. That is why men of high spirit working to regenerate a fallen people must be more insistent to watch every little defect and weak tendency that in a braver time would leave the soul unruffled. That is why every difficulty, once it becomes evident, is ripe for settlement. To evade the issue is to invite disaster. Resolution alone will save us in our many dangers. But a plea for policy will be raised to evade a particular and urgent question : "People won't unite on it"; that's one cry.

"Ignorant people will be led astray"; that's another cry. There is always some excuse ready for evasion. The difficulty is, that every party likes some part of the truth; no party likes it all; but we must have it all, every line of it. We want no popular editions and no philosophic selections— the truth, the whole truth, and nothing but the truth. This must be the rule for everything concerning which a man has a public duty and ought to have a public opinion. There is a dangerous tendency gaining ground of slurring over vital things because the settlement of them involves great difficulty, and may involve great danger; but whatever the issue is we must face it. It is a step forward to bring men together on points of agreement, but men come thus together not without a certain amount of suspicion. In a fight for freedom that latent suspicion would become a mastering fear to seize and destroy us. We must allay it now. We must lead men to discuss points of difference with respect, forbearance, and courage, to find a consistent way of life for all that will inspire confidence in all. At present we inspire confidence in no one; it would be fatal to hide the fact. This is a necessary

D

step to bringing matters to a head. We cannot hope to succeed all at once, but we must keep the great aim in view. There will be objections on all sides; from the *blasé* man of the world, concerned only for his comfort, the mean man of business concerned only for his profits, the man of policy always looking for a middle way, a certain type of religious pessimist who always spies danger in every proposal, and many others. We need not consider the comfort of the first nor the selfishness of the second; but the third and fourth require a word. The man of policy offers me his judgment instead of a clear consideration of the truth. 'Tis he who says : "You and I can discuss certain things privately. We are educated; we understand. Ignorant people can't understand, and you only make mischief in supposing it. It's not wise." To him I reply : "You are afraid to speak the whole truth; I am afraid to hide it. You are filled with the danger to ignorant people of having out everything; I am filled with the danger to *you* of suppressing anything. I do not propose to you that you can with the whole truth make ignorant people profound, but I say you must have the whole truth out for your own salvation." Here is the danger : we see life within certain limitations, and cannot see the possibly infinite significance of something we would put by. It is of grave importance that we see it rightly, and in the difficulties of the case our only safe course is to take the evidence life offers without prejudice and without fear, and write it down. When the matter is grave, let it be taken with all the mature deliberation and care its gravity demands, but once the evidence is clearly seen, let us for our salvation write it down. For any man to set his petty judgment above the need for setting down the truth is madness; and I refuse to do it. There is our religious pessimist to consider. To him I say I take religion more seriously. I take it not to evade the problems of life, but to solve them. When I tell him to have no fear, this is not my indifference to the issue, but a tribute to the faith that is in me. Let us be careful to do the right thing; then fear is inconsistent with faith. Nor can I understand the other attitude. Two thousand years after the preaching of the Sermon on the Mount we are to go about whispering to one another what is wise.

VI

To conclude : Now, and in every phase
of the coming struggle, the strong mind is
a greater need than the strong hand. We
must be passionate, but the mind must
guide and govern our passion. In the
aberrations of the weak mind decrying
resistance, let us not lose our balance and
defy brute strength. At a later stage we
must consider the ethics of resistance to
the Civil Power; the significance of what
is written now will be more apparent then.
Let the cultivation of a brave, high spirit
be our great task; it will make of each
man's soul an unassailable fortress.
Armies may fail, but it resists for ever.
The body it informs may be crushed; the
spirit in passing breathes on other souls,
and other hearts are fired to action, and
the fight goes on to victory. To the man
whose mind is true and resolute ultimate
victory is assured. No sophistry can sap
his resistance; no weakness can tempt
him to savage reprisals. He will neither
abandon his heritage nor poison his
nature. And in every crisis he is steadfast,
in every issue justified. Rejoice, then

good comrades; our souls are still our own. Through the coldness and depression of the time there has lightened a flash of the old fire; the old enthusiasm, warm and passionate, is again stirring us; we are forward to uphold our country's right, to fight for her liberty, and to justify our own generation. We shall conquer. Let the enemy count his dreadnoughts and number off his legions—where are now the legions of Rome and Carthage? And the Spirit of Freedom they challenged is alive and animating the young nations to-day. Hold we our heads high, then, and we shall bear our flag bravely through every fight. Persistent, consistent, straightforward and fearless, so shall we discipline the soul to great deeds, and make it indomitable. In the indomitable soul lies the assurance of our ultimate victory.

CHAPTER IV

I

O UR enemies are brothers from whom we are estranged. Here is the fundamental truth that explains and justifies our hope of re-establishing a real patriotism among all parties in Ireland, and a final peace with our ancient enemy of England. It is the view of prejudice that makes of the various sections of our people hopelessly hostile divisions, and raises up a barrier of hate between Ireland and England that can never be surmounted. If Ireland is to be regenerated, we must have internal unity; if the world is to be regenerated, we must have world-wide unity —not of government, but of brotherhood. To this great end every individual, every nation has a duty; and that the end may

not be missed we must continually turn
for the correction of our philosophy to re-
flecting on the common origin of the
human race, on the beauty of the world
that is the heritage of all, our common
hopes and fears, and in the greatest sense
the mutual interests of the peoples of the
earth. If, unheeding this, any people
make their part of the earth ugly with acts
of tyranny and baseness, they threaten the
security of all; if unconscious of it, a people
always high-spirited are plunged into war
with a neighbour, now a foe, and yet fight,
as their nature compels them, bravely and
magnanimously, they but drive their
enemy back to the field of a purer life, and,
perhaps, to the realisation of a more beautiful existence, a dream to which his
stagnant soul steeped in ugliness could
never rise.

II

On the road to freedom every alliance
will be sternly tried. Internal friendship
will not be made in a day, nor external
friendship for many a day, and there will
be how many temptations to hold it all a
delusion and scatter the few still standing
loyally to the flag. We must understand,

then, the bond that holds us together on the line of march, and in the teeth of every opposition. Nothing but a genuine bond of brotherhood can so unite men, but we hardly seem to realise its truth. When a deep and ardent patriotism requires men of different creeds to come together frankly and in a spirit of comradeship, and when the most earnest of all the creeds do so, others who are colder and less earnest regard this union as a somewhat suspicious alliance; and, if they join in, do so reluctantly. Others come not at all; these think our friends labour in a delusion, that it needs but an occasion to start an old fear and drive them apart, to attack one another with ancient bitterness fired with fresh venom. We must combat that idea. Let us consider the attitude to one another of three units of the band, who represent the best of the company and should be typical of the whole; one who is a Catholic, one who is a Protestant, and one who may happen to be neither. The complete philosophy of any one of the three may not be accepted by the other two; the horizon of his hopes may be more or less distant, but that complete philosophy stretches beyond the limit of the sphere, within which they are drawn together to mutual understanding and comradeship, moved by a common hope, a brave purpose and a beautiful dream. The significance of their work may be deeper for one than for another, the origin of the dream and its ultimate aim may be points not held in common; but the beautiful tangible thing that they all now fight for, the purer public and private life, the more honourable dealings between men, the higher ideals for the community and the nation, the grander forbearance, courage and freedom, in all these they are at one. The instinctive recognition of an attack on the ideal is alive and vigilant in all three. The sympathy that binds them is ardent, deep and enduring. Observe them come together. Note the warm hand grasp, the drawn face of one, a hard-worker; of another, the eye anxious for a brother hard pressed; of the third, the eye glistening for the ideal triumphant; of all the intimate confidence, the mutual encouragement and self-sacrifice, never a note of despair, but always the exultation of the Great Fight, and the promise of a great victory. This is a finer company than a mere casual alliance; yet it makes the uninspired pause, wondering and questioning. These men are earnest men of different creeds; still they are as intimately bound to one another as if they knelt at the one altar. In the narrow view the creeds should be at one another's throats; here ' they are marching shoulder to shoulder. How is this? And the one whose creed is the most exacting could, perhaps, give the best reply. He would reply that within the sphere in which they work together the true thing that unites them can be done only the one right way; that instinctively seizing this right way they come together; that this is the line of advance to wider and deeper things that are his inspiration and his life; that if a comrade is roused to action by the nearer task, and labours bravely and rightly for it, he is on the road to widening vistas in his dream that now he may not see. That is what he would say whose vision of life is the widest. All objectors he may not satisfy. That what is life to him may leave his comrade cold is a difficulty; but against the difficulty stand the depth and reality of their comradeship, proven by mutual sacrifice, endurance, and faith, and he never doubts that their bond union will sometime prove

to have a wise and beautiful meaning in
the Annals of God.

III

But the men of different creeds who
stand firmly and loyally together are a
minority. We are faced with the great
difficulty of uniting as a whole North and
South; and we are faced with the grim fact
that many whom we desire to unite are
angrily repudiating a like desire, that
many are sarcastically noting this, that
many are coldly refusing to believe; while
through it all the most bitter are emphasis-
ing enmity and glorifying it. All these
unbelievers keep insisting North and South
are natural enemies and must so remain.
The situation is further embittered by acts
of enmity being practised by both sides to
the extreme provocation of the faithful
few. Their forbearance will be sorely
tried, and this is the final test of men. By
those who cling to prejudice and abandon
self-restraint, extol enmity, and always
proceed to the further step—the plea to
wipe the enemy out : the counter plea for
forbearance is always scorned as the enervating gospel of weakness and despair.
Though we like to call ourselves Christian,

we have no desire for—nay even make a
jest of—that outstanding Christian virtue;
yet men not held by Christian dogma have
joyously surrendered to the sublimity of
that divine idea. Hear Shelley speak:
" What nation has the example of the deso-
lation of Attica by Mardonius and Xerxes,
or the extinction of the Persian Empire by
Alexander of Macedon restrained from out-
rage? Was not the pretext for this latter
system of spoliation derived immediately
from the former? Had revenge in this in-
stance any other effect than to increase,
instead of diminishing, the mass of malice
and evil already existing in the world?
The emptiness and folly of retaliation are
apparent from every example which can
be brought forward." Shelley writes much
further on retaliation, which he denounces
as " futile superstition." Simple violence repels every high and generous thinker.
Hear one other, Mazzini : " What we have
to do is not to establish a new order of
things by violence. An order of things so
established is always tyrannical even when
it is better than the old." Let us bear this
in mind when there is an act of aggression on either side of the Boyne. There
will not be wanting on the other side a cry

for retaliation and "a lesson." We shall
receive every provocation to give up and
acknowledge ancient bitterness, but then
is the time to stand firm, then we shall need
to practise the divine forbearance that is
the secret of strength.

IV

But with only a minority standing to the
flag we cry out for some hope of final
success. Men will not fight without result
for ever; they ask for some sign of progress, some gleam of the light of victory.
Happily, searching the skies, our eyes can
have their reward. We shall, no doubt,
see, outstanding, dark evidence of old animosity; we shall hear fierce war-cries and
see raging crowds, but the crowds are less
numerous, and the wrath has lost its sting.
Men who raged twenty years ago rage now,
but their fury is less real; and young
men growing up around them, quite
indifferent to the ideal, are also indifferent to the counter cries : they are
passive, unimpressed by either side.
Rightly approached, they may understand
and feel the glow of a fine enthusiasm;
they are numbered by prejudice, they will
become warm, active and daring under an

inspiring appeal. Remember, and have done with despair. Think how you and I found our path step by step of the way : political life was full of conventions that suited our fathers' time, but have faded in the light of our day. We found these conventions unreal and put them by. This was no reflection on our fathers; what they fought for truly is our heritage, and we pay them a tribute in offering it in turn our loyalty inspired by their devotion. But their errors we must rectify; what they left undone we must take up and fulfil. That is the task of every generation, to take up the uncompleted work of the former one, and hand on to their successors an achievement and a heritage. Youth recognises this instinctively, and every generation will take a step in advance of its predecessor, putting by its prejudices and developing its truth. Every individual may know this from his own experience, and from it he knows that those who are now voicing old bitter cries are ageing, and will soon pass and leave no successors. Not that prejudice will die for ever. Each new day will have its own, but that which is now dividing and hampering us will pass. Let the memory of its bitter-

ness be an incentive to checking new
animosities and keeping the future safe;
but in the present let us grasp and keep
in our mind that the barrier that sun-
dered our nation must crumble, if only
we have faith and persist, undeterred
by old bitter cries, for they are dying
cries, undepressed by millions apathetic,
for it is the great recurring sign of the
ideal, that one hour its light will flash
through quivering multitudes, and millions will have vision and rouse to re-
generate the land.

v

Happily, it is nothing new to plead for
brotherhood among Irishmen now; unhappily, it is not so generally admitted, nor
even recognised, that the same reason
that exists for restoring friendly relations
among Irishmen, exists for the re-establishing of friendship with any outsider—
England or another—with whom now or
in the future we may be at war. Friendli-
ness between neighbours is one of the
natural things of life. In the case of individuals how beautifully it shows between
two dwellers in the same street or townland.
They rejoice together in prosperity; give

mutual aid in adversity; in the ordinary
daily round work together in a spirit of
comradeship; at all times they find a bond
of unity in their mutual interests. Consider, then, the sundering of their friendship by some act of evil on either side.
The old friendship is turned to hate. Now
the proximity that gave intimate pleasure
to their comradeship gives as keen an edge
to their enmity; they meet one another,
cross one another, harass one another at
every point. The bitterness that is such a
poison to life must be revolting to their
best instincts; deep in their hearts must be
a yearning for the casting out of hate and
the return of old comradeship. Still the
estranged brothers are at daggers drawn.
Sometimes the evil done is so great and
the bitterness so keen that the old spirit can
apparently never be restored; but while
there is any hope whatever the true heart
will keep it alive deep down, for it must
be cherished and kept in mind if the whole
beauty of life is to be renewed and preserved for ever. It is so with nations as
with individuals. Once this is recognised
we must be on guard against a new error,
which is an old error in new form, the
taking of means for end. The end of

general peace is to give all nations freedom in essentials, to realise the deeper purpose, possibilities, fulness and beauty of life; it is not to have a peace at any price, peace with a certain surrender, the meaner peace that is akin to slavery. No, its message is to guard one nation from excess that has plunged another into evil, to leave the way open to a final peace, not base but honourable; it is to preserve the divine balance of the soul. It may be further urged that we are engaged in a great fight; that to try to rouse in men the more generous instincts will but weaken their hands by removing a certain driving bitterness that gives strength to their fight. Whatever it removes it will not be their strength. In a war admittedly between brothers, a civil war, where different conceptions of duty force men asunder, father is up against son, and brother against brother; yet they are not weakened in their contest by ties of blood and the deeper-lying harmony of things that in happier times prevail to the exclusion of bitterness and hate. When, therefore, you teach a man his enemy is in a deep sense his brother, you do not draw him from the fight, but you give him a new conception of the goal to win and with

E

a great dream inspire him to persevere and reach the goal.

VI

If, then, beyond individual and national freedom there is this great dream still to be striven for, let us not decry it as something too sublime for earth. It must be our guiding star to lead us rightly as far as we may go. We can travel rightly that part of the road we now tread on only by shaping it true to the great end that ought to inspire us all. We shall have many temptations to swerve aside, but the power of mind that keeps our position clear and firm will react against every destroying influence. In the first stage of the fight for internal unity, when blind ˙bigotry is furiously insisting that we but plan an insidious scheme for the oppression of a minority, our firmness will save us till our conception of the end grow on that minority and convince all of our earnestness. Then the dream will inspire them, the flag will claim them, and the first stage in the fight will be won. When internal unity is accomplished, we are within reach of freedom. Yes, but cries an objector, "Why plead for friendship with England, who will have peace only on condition of her supremacy?" And an answer is needed. If it takes two to make a fight, it also most certainly takes two to make a peace, unless one accepts the position of serf and surrenders. But this we do not fear; we can compel our freedom and we are confident of victory. There is still the step to friendship. Many will be baffled by the difficulty, that while we must keep alive our generous instincts, we must be stern and resolute in the fight; while we desire peace we must prosecute war; while we long for comradeship we must be breaking up dangerous alliances : literary, political, trades and social unions formed with England while she is asserting her supremacy must be broken up till they can be reformed on a basis of independence, equality and universal freedom. While we are prosecuting these vigorous measures it may not seem the way to final friendship; but we must persist; independence is first indispensable. Here again, however, while insisting among our own ranks on our conception of the end, it will grow on the mind of the enemy. They may put it by at first as a delusion or a snare, but one intimate moment will come when it will light up for them, and a new

era is begun. In such a moment is evil
abandoned, hate buried and friendship re-
born. There is one honest fear that
our independence would threaten their
security : it will yet be replaced by the
conviction that there is a surer safeguard
in our freedom than in our suppression;
the light will break through the clouds of
suspicion and a star of stars will glorify
the earth. For this end our enemy must
have an ideal as high as our own; if thus
an objector, he is right. But if in the gross
materialism and greed of empire that is
now the ruling passion with the enemy
there is apparently little hope of a transformation that will make them spiritual,
high-minded and generous, we must not
abandon our ideal : while the meanness
and tyranny of contemporary England
stand forward against our argument and
leave our reasoning cold, we can find a
more subtle appeal in spirit, such an
appeal as comes to us in a play of Shakespeare's, a song of Shelley's, or a picture
of Turner's. From the heart of the enemy
Genius cries, bearing witness to our
common humanity, and the yearning for
such high comradeship is alive, and the
dream survives to light us on the forward

path.   We must travel that path rightly.
We can so travel whatever the enemy's
mind.   More difficult it will be, but it can
be done.   That is the great significance
and justification of Nationalism : it is the
unanswerable argument to cosmopolitan-
ism.   If the greatness and beauty of life
that ought to be the dream of all nations
is denied by all but one, that one may keep
alive the dream within her own frontier
till its fascination will arrest and inspire
the world.   If this ultimate dream is still
floating far off, in its pursuit there is for
us achievement on achievement, and each
brave thing done is in itself a beauty and
a joy for ever.   For the good fighter there
is always fine recompense; a clear mind,
warm blood, quick imagination, grasp of
life and joy in action, and at the end of
day always an eminence won.   Yes, and
from the height of that eminence will
come ringing down to the last doubter a
last word : we may reach the mountain-
tops in aspiring to the stars.

CHAPTER V

THE SECRET OF STRENGTH

I

TO win our freedom we must be strong. But what is the secret of strength? It is fundamental to the whole question to understand this rightly, and, once grasped, make it the mainstay of individual existence, which is the foundation of national life. So much has the bodily power of over-riding minorities been made the criterion of absolute power, that to make clear the truth requires patience, insight, and a little mental study. But the end is a great end. It is to reconnoitre the most important battlefield, to discover the dispositions of the enemy, to measure our own resources and forge our strength

link by link till we put on the armour of
invincibility.

II

We have to grasp a distinction, knowledge of which is essential to discerning
true strength. It can be clearly seen in
the contrast between two certain fighting
forces; first, a well-organised army, cap-
ably led, marching forward full of hope
and buoyancy; second, a remnant of that
army after disaster, a mere handful, not
swept like their comrades in panic, but
with souls set to fight a forlorn hope. Let
us study the two : in the contrast we shall
learn the secret. The courage of the well-
organised army is not of so fine a quality
as that nerving the few to fight to the last
gasp. Consider first the army. What is
its value as a force? Its discipline, its
consolidation, the absolute obedience of
its units to its officers, with the resulting
unity of the whole; added to this is the
sense of security in numbers, buoyancy
of marching in a compact body, confidence
in capable chiefs—all these factors go to
the making of the courage and strength
of the army. It is because their combination makes for the reliability of the force

that discipline is so much valued and en-
forced, even to the point of death. Let us
keep this in our mind, that their strength
lies in their numbers, concentration,
unity, reliance on one another and on
their chiefs. A sudden disaster overtakes
that army—the death of a great general,
the miscarriage of some plan, a surprise
attack, any of the chances of war, and the
strength of the army is pierced, the discipline shaken, the sense of security gone.
There is an instinctive movement to retreat;
the habit of discipline keeps it orderly
at first; the fear grows; all precaution and
restraint are thrown aside—the retreat is
a rout, the army a rabble, the end debacle.
External discipline in giving them its
strength left them without individual resource; internal discipline was ignored.
When their combined strength was gone
there was individual helplessness and
panic. Consider, now, a remnant of that
army, the members of which have the
courage of the finer quality, individually
resolute and set on resistance, clearly
seeing at once all the possible consequences of their action, yet with that
higher quality of soul accepting them
without hesitation, pledging all human

hopes for one last great hope of snatching victory from defeat, or, if not to save a lost battle, to check an advancing host, rally flying forces, and redeem a campaign. This is the heroic quality. In a crisis, the mind possessed of it does not wait for instructions or to reason a conclusion. It sees definite things, and swift as thought decides. There are flying legions, a flag down, a conquering army, and flight or death—to all eyes these are apparent; but to a brave company between that flight and death there is a gleam of hope, of victory, and for that forlorn hope flight is put by with the acceptance of death in the alternative if they fail. That is the quality to redeem us. Because it is witnessed so often in our history we are going to win; not for our prowess in more fortunate war on an even field or with the flowing tide, not for many victories in many lands, but for the sacred places in this our brave land that are memorable for fights that registered the land unconquerable. Why a last stand and a sacrifice are more inspiring than a great victory is one of the hidden things; but the truth stands : for thinking of them our spirits re-kindle, our courage reawakens, and we stiffen our backs for another battle.

III

We have, then, to develop individual patience, courage, and resolution. Once this is borne in mind our work begins. In places there is a dangerous idea that sometime in the future we may be called on to strike a blow for freedom, but in the meantime there is little to do but watch and wait. This is a fatal error; we have to forge our strength in the interval. There is a further mistake that our national work is something apart, that social, business, religious and other concerns have no relation to it, and consequently we set apart a few hours of our leisure for national work, and go about our day as if no nation existed. But the middle of the day has a natural connection with the beginning of the day and the end of the day, and in whatever sphere a man finds himself, his acts must be in relation to and consistent with every other sphere. He will be the best patriot and the best soldier who is the best friend and the best citizen. One cannot be an honest man in one sphere and a rascal in another; and since a citizen to fulfil his duty to his country must be honourable and zealous, he must develop the underlying virtues in private life. He must strengthen the individual character, and to do this he must deal with many things seemingly remote and inconsequential from a national point of view. Everything that crosses a man's path in his day's round of little or great moment requires of him an attitude towards it, and the conscious or unconscious shaping of his attitude is determining how he will proceed in other spheres not now in view. Suppose the case of a man in business or social life. He has to work with others in a day's routine or fill up with them hours of leisure they enjoy together. Consider to what accompaniment the work is often done and with what manner of conversation the leisure is often filled. In a day's routine, where men work together, harmonious relations are necessary; yet what bickerings, contentions, animosities fill many a day over points never worth a thought. You will see two men squabble like cats for the veriest trifle, and then go

through days like children, without a
word. You will see something similar in
social life among men and women equally
—petty jealousies, personalities, slander-
ings, mean little stories of no great
consequence in themselves, except in the
converse sense of showing how small and
contemptible everything and everyone
concerned is. A keen eye notes with some
depression the absence from both spheres
of a fine manliness, a generous conception
of things, a large outlook, that prevents a
squabble with a smile, and because of a
consciousness of the need for determination in a great fight for a principle, holds
in true contempt the trivialities of an
hour. For in all the mean little bickerings
of life there is involved not a principle, but
a petty pride. One has to note these things
and decide a line of action. In the abstract
the right course seems quite natural and
easy, but in fact it is not so. A man finds
another act towards him with unconscious
impudence or arrogance, and at once flies
into a rage; there is a fierce wrangle, and
at the end he finds no purpose served, for
nothing was at stake. He has lost his
temper for nothing. In his heat he may
tell you " he wouldn't let so-and-so do so-

and-so," but on the same principle he should hold a street-argument with every fish-wife who might call him a name. He may tell you "he will make so-and-so respect him," but he offends his own self-respect if he cannot consider some things beneath him. One must have a sense of proportion and not elevate every little act of impudence into a challenge of life to be fought over as for life and death. It may be corrected with a little humour or a little disdain, but always with sympathy for the narrow mind whose view of life cannot reach beyond these petty things. Yet, to repeat, it is not easy. An irritable temper will be on fire before reason can check it; the process of correction will prove uncomfortable—the reasons will be there, but the feelings in revolt. Still, little by little, it is brought under, and in the end the nasty little irritability is killed just like a troublesome nerve; and, by and by, what once provoked a fierce rage becomes a subject for humorous reflection. Let no one fear we kill the nerve for the great Battle of Life; this we but strengthen and make constant. Every act of personal discipline is contributing to a subconscious reservoir whence our nobler energies are supplied for ever. And so, little things lead to great; and in an office wrangle or a social squabble there is need for developing those very qualities of judgment, courage, and patience which equip a man for the trials of the battlefield or the ruling of the state.

IV

We have considered the individual in business and social life. Let us now follow him into a political assembly. We find the same conditions prevail. Again, men fight bitterly but most frequently for nothing worth a fight; and again those rightly judging the situation must resolve not to be tempted into a wrangle even if their restraint be called by another name. What in a political assembly is often the first thing to note? We begin by the assumption, "this is a practical body of men," the words invariably used to cover the putting by of some great principle that we ought all endorse and uphold. But, first, by one of the many specious reasons now approved, we put the principle by, and before long we are at one another's throats about things involving no principle. It is not necessary to particularise. Note any meeting for the same general conditions : a chairman, indecisive, explaining rules of order which he lacks the grit to apply; members ignoring the chair and talking at one another; others calling to order or talking out of time or away from the point; one unconsciously showing the futility of the whole business by asking occasionally what is before the chair, or what the purpose of the meeting. This picture is familiar to us all, and curiously we seem to take it always as the particular freak of a particular time or locality; but it is nothing of the kind. It is the natural and logical result of putting by principle and trying to live away from it. Yet, that is what we are doing every day. It means we lack collectively the courage to pursue a thing to its logical conclusion and fight for the truth realised. If we are to be otherwise as a body, it will only be by personal discipline training for the wider and greater field. We must get a proper conception of the great cause we stand for, its magnitude and majesty, and that to be worthy of its service we must have a standard above reproach, have an end of petty proposals and underhand doings, be of brave front, resolute heart, and honourable intent. We must all understand this each in his own mind and shape his actions, each to be found faithful in the test. In fine, if in private life there is need for developing the great virtues requisite for public service, even more is it necessary in public life to develop the courage, patience and wisdom of the soldier and the statesman.

V

A concrete case will give a clearer grasp of the issue than any abstract reasoning. Our history, recent and remote, affords many examples of the abandoning by our public men of a principle, to defend which they entered public life; and our action on such an occasion is invariably the same—to regard the delinquent as simply a traitor, to load him with invective and scorn and brand him for ever. We never see it is not innate wickedness in the man, but a weakness against which he has been untrained and undisciplined, and which leaves him helpless in the first crisis. Ireland has recently been incensed by the

action of some of her mayors and lord
mayors in connection with the English
Coronation festival; the feeling has been
acute in the metropolis. Certain things
are obvious, but how many see what is
below the surface? Let me suggest a case
and a series of circumstances; the more
pointed the case, the more interesting. I
will suppose a particular mayor is an old
Fenian : let us see how for him a web is
finely woven, and in the end how securely
he is netted. First a mayor is a magistrate, and must take the judicial oath, but
the old Fenian has taken an oath of
allegiance to Ireland—clash number one.
It is not simply a question of yes or
no; there are attendant circumstances.
Around a public man in place circulates a
swarm of interested people, needy friends,
meddling politicians, " supporters" generally. The chief magistrate will have influence on the bench which they all wish
to invoke now and then, and they all wish
to see him there. They don't approve of
any principle that stands in the way.
They group themselves together as his
" supporters," and claiming to have put
him into public life, they act as if they
had acquired a lease of his soul. Not what

F

he knows to be right, but what they believe to be useful, must be done; and before the first day is done the first fight must be made. However, the old Fenian has enough of the spirit of old times to come safe through the first round. But the second is close on his heels : Dublin Castle has been attentive. The mayor, as chief magistrate, has privileges on which the Castle now silently closes. There are private and veiled remonstrances by secret officials : "The mayor is acting illegally; he must not do so-and-so; such is the function of a magistrate; he has not taken the oath," etc. All this renewing the fight of the first day, for the Castle, too, wants the mayor on the bench to brand him as its own and alienate him from the old flag. It puts on the pressure by suppressing his privileges, weakening his influence, and disappointing his "supporters." All this is silently done. Still, the mayor holds fast, but he has not counted on this, and is beginning to be baffled and worried. Meanwhile a sort of guerilla attack is being maintained : invitations arrive to garden parties at Windsor, lesser functions nearer home, free passages to all the gay festivals, free admissions everywhere, the route indicated, and a gracious request for the presence of the mayor and mayoress. Genuine business engagements now save the situation, and the invitations are put by, but our chief citizen is now bewildered. These social missiles are flying in all directions, always gracious and flattering, never challenging and rude—who can withstand them? Still he is bewildered, but not yet caught. A new assault is made : the great Health Crusade Battery is called up. Here we must all unite, God's English and the wild Irish, the Fenian and the Castleman, the labourer and the lord. Surely, we are all against the microbes. There is a great demonstration, their Excellencies attend—and the mayor presides. Under the banner of the microbe he is caught. It is a great occasion, which their Excellencies grace and improve. His Excellency is affable with the mayor; her Excellency is confidential and gracious with the mayoress—we might have been schoolchildren in the same townland we are so cordial. Everything proceeds amid plaudits, and winds up in acclamation. Their Excellencies depart. Great is the no-politics era—you can so quietly spike the guns of many an old politician—and keep

him safe. The social amenities do this.
Their Excellencies have gone, but they do
not forget. There is a warm word of
thanks for recent hospitality. Perhaps the
mayor has a daughter about to be married,
or a son has died; it is remembered, and
the cordial congratulation or gracious
sympathy comes duly under the great seal.
What surly man would resent sympathy?
And so, the strength of the old warrior is
sapped; the web is woven finely; in its
secret net the Castle has its man. You who
have exercised yourselves in Dublin recently over mayoral doings, note all this—
not to the making light of any man's surrender, but to the true judging of the
event, its deeper significance and danger.
Whoever fails must be called to account.
When a man takes a position of trust, influence, and honour, and, whatever the
difficulty, abandons a principle he should
hold sacred, he must be held responsible.
A battle is an ordeal, and we must be stern
with friend and foe. But there is something more sinister than the weakness of
the man : remember the net.

VI

The concrete case makes clear the principle in question. The man whom we have seen go down would have been safe if he had to fight no battle but one he could face with all his true friends, and in the open light of day. Having to fight a secret battle was never even considered : threats direct or vague or subtle, blandishments, cajolery, graciousness, patronage, flattery, plausible generalities, attacks indirect and insidious —all coming without pause, secret, silent, tireless. He who is to be proof against this, and above threat or flattery, must have been disciplined with the discipline of a life that trains him for every emergency. You cannot take up such a character like a garment to suit the occasion : it must be developed in private and public by all those daily acts that declare a man's attitude, register his convictions, and form his mind. It gives its own reward at once, even in the day where nothing is apparently at stake; where men scramble furiously over the petty things of life; for he who sees these things at their proper value is unruffled. His composure in all the fury has its own value. But the mind that held him so, by the very act of dismissing something petty, gets a clearer conception of the great things of life; by intuition is at once awake to a hovering and fatal menace to individual or national existence, unseen of the common eye; and in that hour proves, to the confusion of the enemy, clear, vigorous and swift. Let us, then, for this great end note what is the secret of strength. Not alone to be ready to stand in with a host and march bravely to battle—the discipline that provides for this is great and valuable and must be always observed and practised. This gives, however, only the common courage of the crowd, and can only be trusted on an even field where the chances of war are equal. But when there is a struggle to restore freedom, where from the nature of the case the chances are uneven and the soldiers of liberty are at every disadvantage, then must we seek to adjust the balance by a finer courage and a more enduring strength. The mustering of legions will not suffice. The general reviewing this fine array who would rightly estimate the power he may command, must silently examine the units, to judge of this brave host how large a company can be formed to fight a forlorn hope.   If this spirit is in reserve, he is armed against every emergency.   If the chances are equal, he will have a splendid victory; if by any of the turns of war his legions are shaken and disaster threatened, there is always a certain rallying-ground where the host can re-form and the field be re-won, and the flag that has seen so many vicissitudes be set at last high and proudly in the light of Freedom.

CHAPTER VI

PRINCIPLE IN ACTION

I

OUR philosophy is valueless unless we bring it into life. With sufficient ingenuity we might frame theory after theory, and if they could not be put to the test of a work-a-day existence we but add another to the many dead theories that litter the History of Philosophy. Our principles are not to argue about, or write about, or hold meetings about, but primarily to give us a rule of life. To ignore this is to waste time and energy. To observe and follow it is to take from the clouds something that appeals to us, work it into life, by it interpret the problems to hand, make our choice between opposing standards, and maintain our fidelity to the true one against every opposition and through every fitful though terrible depression; so shall we startle people with its reality, and make for it a disciple or an opponent, but always at once convince the generation that there is a serious work in hand.

II

If our philosophy is to be worked into life the first thing naturally is to review the situation. If we are to judge rightly, we must understand the present, draw from the past its lesson, and shape our plans for the future true to the principles that govern and inform every generation. Let us survey the past, taking a sufficiently wide view between two points—say '98 and our own time—and we see certain definite conditions. Great luminous years —'98, '03, '48, '67, rise up, witness to a great principle, readiness for sacrifice, unshaken belief in truth, valour and freedom, and a flag that will ultimately prevail. In these years the people had vision, the blood quickened, a living flame swept the land, scorching up hypocrisy, deceit, meanness, and lighting all brave hearts to high hope and achievement—for, the whimperers notwithstanding, it was always achievement to challenge the enemy and stagger his power, though yet his expulsion is delayed. Between the glorious years of the living flame there intervened pallid times of depression, where every disease of soul and body crept into the open. True hearts lived, scattered here and there, believing still but disorganised and bewildered—the leaders were stricken down and in their place, obscuring the beauty of life, the grandeur of the past, and our future destiny, came time-servers, flatterers, hypocrites, open traffickers in honour and public decency, fastening their mean authority on the land. These are the two great resting-places in our historic survey : the generation of the living flame and the generation of despair; and it is for us to decide—for the decision rests with us— whether we shall in our time merely mark time or write another luminous chapter in the splendid history of our race.

III

Let us consider these two generations apart, to understand their distinctive features more clearly for our own guidance. Take first the years of vision and the general effort to replant the old flag on our walls. With the first enthusiasts breathing the living flame abroad, the kindling hope, the widening fires, the deepening dream, there grows a consciousness of the greatness of the goal, of the general duty, of the individual responsibility for higher character, steadier work, and purer motive; and gradually meanness, trickeries, and treacheries are weeded out of the individual and national consciousness : there is a realisation of a time come to restore the nation's independence, and with passion and enthusiasm are fused a fine resolve and nerve. All the excited doings of the feverish or pallid years are put by as unworthy or futile. The great idea inspires a great fight; and that fight is made, and, notwithstanding any reverse, must be recorded great. Whatever concourse of circumstances mar the dream and delay the victory, those brave years are as a torch in witness to the ideal, in justification of its soldiers and in promise of final success.

IV

Let us examine now the deadening years that intervene between the great fights for freedom. We have known something of these times ourselves, have touched on

them already, and need not further draw
out the demoralising things that corrupt
and dishearten us. But what we urgently
require to study is the kind of effort—more
often the absence of effort—made in such
years by those who keep their belief in
freedom and feel at times impelled in some
way or other to action. They have followed a lost battle, and in the aftermath
of defeat they are numbed into despair.
They refuse to surrender to the forces of
the hour, but they lack the fine faith and
enthusiasm of the braver years that challenged these forces at every point and stood
or fell by the issue. They lie apathetic
till, moved by some particular meanness
or treachery, they are roused to spasmodic
anger, rush to act in some spasmodic way
—generally futile, and then relapse into
helplessness again. They lack the vision
that inspires every moment, discerns a
sure way, and heightens the spirit to battle
without ceasing, which is characteristic of
the great years. They tacitly accept that
theirs is a useless generation, that the
enemy is in the ascendant, that they cannot unseat him, and their action, where
any is made, is but to show their attitude,
never to convince opponents that the battle

is again beginning, that this is a bid for
freedom, that history will be called on to
record their fight and pay tribute to their
times. Their action has never this great
significance. When stung to fitful madness by the boastful votaries of power, their
occasional frantic efforts are more as relief to their feelings than destructive to
the tyranny in being. Let us realise this
to the full; and seeing the futility in other
years of every pathetic makeshift to annoy
or circumvent the enemy, put by futilities
and do a great work to justify our time.

V

We have, then, to consider and decide
our immediate attitude to life, where we
stand. There are errors to remove. The
first is the assumption that we are only
required to acknowledge the flag in places,
offer it allegiance at certain meetings at
certain times that form but a small part
of our existence; while we allow ourselves
to be dispensed from fidelity to our principles when in other places, where other
standards are either explicitly or tacitly
recognised. That we must carry our flag
everywhere; that there must be no dispen-
sation : these are the cardinal points of our

philosophy. Life is a great battlefield, and
any hour in the day a man's flag may be
challenged and he must stand and justify
it. An idea you hold as true is not to be
professed only where it is proclaimed; it
will whisper and you must be its prophet
in strange places; it is insistent of all
things—you must glory in it or deny it;
there is no escaping it, and there is no
middle way; wherever your path lies it
will cross you and you must choose.

Beware lest on any plea you put it by.
You cannot elect to do nothing; the concourse of circumstances would take you to
some side; to do nothing is still to take a
side. Priest, poet, professor, public man,
professional man, business man, tradesman—everyone will be called to answer;
in every walk of life the true idea will find
the false in conflict and the battle must be
fought out there—the battle is lost when
we satisfy ourselves with an academic debate in our spare moments. This is a
debating club age, and a plea for an ideal
is often wasted, taken as a mere point in
an argument; but to walk among men
fighting passionately for it as a thing believed in, is to make it real, to influence
men never reached in other ways; it is to

arrest attention, arouse interest and quicken the masses to advance. And wherever the appeal for the flag is calling us the snare of the enemy is in wait. Our history so bristles with instances that a particular concrete case need not be cited. We know that priests will get more patronage if they discourage the national idea; that professors will get more emoluments and honours if they can ban it; that public men will receive places and titles if they betray it; that the professional man will be promised more aggrandisement, the business man more commerce, and the tradesman more traffic of his kind—if only he put by the flag. Most treacherous and insidious the temptation will come to the man, young and able, everywhere. It will say, "You have ability; come into the light —only put that by; it keeps you obscure. And what purpose does it serve now? Be practical; come." And you may weaken and yield and enter the light for the general applause, but the old idea will rankle deep down till smothered out, and you will stand in the splendour—a failure, miserable, hopeless, not apparent, indeed, but for all that, final. You may stand your ground, refuse the bribe, uphold the flag, and be rated a fool and a failure, but they who rate you so will not understand that you have won a battle greater than all the triumphs of empires; you will keep alive in your soul true light and enduring beauty; you will hear the music eternally in the heart of the high enthusiast and have vision of ultimate victory that has sustained all the world over the efforts of centuries, that uplifts the individual, consolidates the nation, and leads a wandering race from the desert into the Promised Land.

VI

If we are to justify ourselves in our time we must have done with dispensations. Many honest men are astray on this point and think attitudes justifiable that are at the root of all our failures. What is the weakness? It is so simple to explain and so easy to understand that one must wonder how we have been ignoring it quietly and generally so long. A man, as we have seen, acknowledges his flag in certain places; in other places it is challenged and he pulls it down. He is dispensed. He believes in his heart, may even write an anonymous letter to the paper, will salute the flag again elsewhere, but he will not carry his flag through every fight and through every day. When a particular crisis arises, which involves our public boards, public men, and business men in action, that requires a decision for or against the nation, he will find it in his place in life not wise to be prominent on his own side, and he is silently absent from his meetings—he gives a subscription but excuses himself from attendance. He satisfies himself with private professions of faith and whispered encouragement to those who fill the gap—words that won't be heard at a distance—and, worst of all, he thinks, because some stake in life may be jeopardised by bolder action, he is justified. The answer is, simply he is not justified. Nor should anyone who is prepared to take the risk himself take it on himself to absolve others—nor, least of all, openly preach a milder doctrine to lead others who are timid to the farther goal, believed in at heart. Encourage them by all means to practise their principles as far as they go; never restrict yours, or you will find yourself saying things you can't altogether approve; and if you tell a man to do things you can't altogether approve, and keep on telling him, it wears into you, and

G

a thing you once held in abhorrence you
come to think of with indifference. You
change insensibly. Old friends rage at
you, and because of it you rage at them—
not knowing how you have changed. You
dare not let what you believe lie in abey-
ance or say things inconsistent with it, else
to-morrow you'll be puzzled to say what
you believe. You will hardly say two
things to fit each other. Let us have no
half policies. Our policy must be full,
clear, consistent, to satisfy the restless, inquiring minds; when we win all such over,
the merely passive people will follow. It
should be clear that no man can dispense
himself or his fellow from a grave duty;
but for all that we have been liberal with
our dispensations, and it has left us in confusion and failure. On the understanding
that we will be heroes to-morrow, we
evade being men to-day. We think of
some hazy hour in the future when we
may get a call to great things; we realise
not that the call is now, that the fight is
afoot, that we must take the flag from its
hidden resting-place and carry it boldly
into life. So near a struggle may touch us
with dread; but to dread provoking a fight
is to endure without resistance all the con-

sequences of a lost battle—a battle that might have been won. And if we are to be fit for the heroic to-morrow we must arise and be men to-day.

VII

At times we find ourselves on neutral ground. The exigencies of the struggle involve this; and unfortunately we have in our midst sincere men who do not believe in restoring Ireland to her original independence. Perhaps, from a tendency to lose our balance at times, it is well to have near by these men whose obvious sincerity may serve as a correcting influence. We have to make them one with us; in the meantime we meet them on neutral ground for some common purpose. Yet, we must take our flag everywhere? Yes, that is fundamental. What then of the places where men of diverging views meet; do we abjure the flag? By no means. The understanding here is not to force our views on others, but we must keep our principles clear in mind that no hostile view be forced on us. We must see to it that neutrality be observed. One of the pitfalls to be aware of is, that something which on our principles we should not recognise, is assumed as recognised by others because to attack it would be to violate neutrality. But if it may not be resisted, it may not be recognised; this is neutrality; it is to stand on equal terms. And since grave matters divide us—not directly concerned in our national struggle for freedom—let the dangerous idea be banished, that in entering on common ground we decry all opposing beliefs. For men who hold beliefs as vital it would not be creditable to either side to put them easily by. No, we do not ask them to forget themselves, but to respect one another— an entirely greater and more honourable principle. On neutral ground a man is not called on to abjure his flag; rather he and his flag are in sanctuary.

VIII

When we find the national idea touches life at every point, we begin to realise how frequent the call is to defend it without warning. It is not that men directly raise the idea purposely to reject it, but that their habit of life, to which they expect all to conform, is unconsciously assuming that our ruling principle can have no place now or in the future. Their assumption that the *status quo* cannot be changed will be the cause of most collision at first; and we must be quietly ready with the counter-assumption, stand for the old idea and justify it. We must realise, too, that the number of people who have definite, strong, well-developed views against ours are comparatively small. This small number embraces the English Government that commands forces, obeying it without reason, and influencing the general mass of people whose general attitude is indecision —adrift with the ruling force. It is this general mass of men we must permeate with the true idea, and give them more decision, more courage, more pride of race, and bring them to prove worthy of the race. They will begin to have confidence in the Cause when they begin to see it vindicated amongst them day by day; and that vindication must be our duty. That duty will not be to seek; it will offer itself and we shall have our test. How! Consider when men come together for any purpose where different views prevail and general things of no great moment form the subject of debate—suddenly, unconsciously or tentatively, one will raise some idea that may divide the company—say, acknowledging the English Crown in Ireland, putting by the claim for freedom, in the foolish hope of some material gain. There is much nonsense talked and confusion abroad on this head, and it is quite possible a man, believing in Ireland's full claim, will find himself in a large company who ought to stand for Ireland, yet who have lost a clear conception of her rights. But he will find that they have no clear conception the other way, either; they are confused and generally pliable; and so, when the challenging idea is introduced, if he is quick and clear with the vital points, he can tear the surface off the many nostrums of the hour and prove them mean, worthless, and degrading; and, doing so, he will be forming the minds about him. He must be ready; that is the great need. Understand how a conversation is often turned by a chance word, and how governed by one man who has passionate, well-defined views, while others are cold and undecided. Be that one man. You do not know where the circumstances of life will take you; your flag may be directly challenged to your face, and you must reveal yourself. These are things to avoid. Be firm, rather than aggressive;

but be always quietly prepared for the aggressive man; that is to inspire confidence in the timid. Avoid vituperation as a disease, but have your facts clear and ready for friend or foe. Whenever, and wherever least expected, a false idea comes wandering forth, put in at once a luminous word or two to clear the air, hearten friends and keep them steady. If you find yourself alone in the midst of opponents, who assume you are with them and expect your co-operation, you put them right with a word. This will arrest them; they will understand where you stand, and that you are ready; and they will generally yield you respect. But whether it involve a fight or not, thus do you declare your attitude. We may conveniently call it—putting up the flag.

IX

It is well to consider something of the opposition that confronts a man who tries to fill his life with a brave purpose. He will be told it is an illusion; he is a dreamer, a crank, or a fool. And it may serve a purpose to see if our critics are blinded by no illusion, to contrast our folly with their wisdom. Here is one

pushing by who will not be a fool, as he
thinks—he's for the emigrant-ship. Ask
yourself if the people who go out from the
remote places of Ireland, quiet-spoken and
ruddy-faced, and return after a few years
loud-voiced and pallid, have found things
exactly as their hope. They protest, yes;
but their voice and colour belie them.
Take the other man who does not emigrate
but who has his fling at home, who
"knocks around" and tells you to do likewise and be no fool—mark him for your
guidance. You will find his leisure is bois-
terous, but never gay. Catch him between
whiles off his guard and you will find the
deadening lassitude of his life. This votary
of pleasure has a burden to carry in whatever walk of life, high or low. On the
higher plane he may have a more fastidious club or two, a more epicurean sense
of enjoyment, more leisure and more
luxury; but the type wherever found is the
same. Life is an utter burden to him; in
his soul is no interest, no inspiration, no
energy, and no hope. Let him be no object
of envy. Here a friend pats you on the
shoulder : " Quite right; be neither an
emigrant nor a waster; but be practical;
have no illusions; deal with possibilities

—who can say what is in the future? We must face these facts." Our confident friend lacks a sense of humour. He would put your plan by for its bearing on the future, but he proposes one himself that the future must justify. He tells you circumstances will not be in your favour : he assumes them in his own. But we only claim that our principles will rule the future as they have ruled the past; for the circumstances no man can speak. He calls you a dreamer for your principles, but he can't show, now nor in history, that his exemplars were ever justified. We are all dreamers, then; but some have ugly dreams, while the dreams of others are beautiful worlds, star-lighted and full of music.

X

Let the newborn enthusiast, just come eagerly to the flag, be warned of hours of depression that seize even the most earnest, the boldest and the strongest. Our work is the work of men, subject to such vicissitudes as hover around all human enterprise; and every man enrolled must face hard struggles and dark hours. Then the depression rushes down like a horrible, cold, dark mist that obscures every beautiful thing and every ray of hope. It may come from many causes: perhaps, a body not too robust, worn down by a tireless mind; perhaps, the memory of long years of effort, seemingly swallowed in oblivion and futility; perhaps contact with men on your own side whose presence there is a puzzle, who have no character and no conception of the grandeur of the Cause, and whose mean, petty, underhand jealousies numb you— you who think anyone claiming so fine a flag as ours should be naturally brave, straightforward and generous; perhaps the seemingly overwhelming strength of the enemy, and the listlessness of thousands who would hail freedom with rapture, but who now stand aloof in despair—and along with all this and intensifying it, the voice of our self-complacent practical friend, who has but sarcasm for a high impulse, and for an immutable principle the latest expedient of the hour. Through such an experience must the soldier of freedom live. But as surely as such an hour comes, there comes also a star to break the darkened sky; let those who feel the battle-weariness at times remember. When in places there may be but one or

two to fight, it may seem of no avail; still
let them be true and their numbers will
be multiplied : love of truth is infectious.
When progress is arrested, don't brood on
what is, but on what was once achieved,
what has since survived, and what we
may yet achieve. If some have grown
lax and temporise a little, with more firmness on your part mingle a little sympathy
for them. It is harder to live a consistent
life than die a brave death. Most men of
generous instincts would rouse all their
courage to a supreme moment and die for
the Cause; but to rise to that supreme
moment frequently and without warning
is the burden of life for the Cause; and it
is because of its exhausting strain and
exacting demands that so many men have
failed. We must get men to realise that to
live is as daring as to die. But confusion
has been made in our time by the glib
phrase : "You are not asked now to die
for Ireland, but to live for her," without
insisting that the life shall aim at the
ideal, the brave and the true. To slip
apologetically through existence is not
life. If such a mean philosophy went
abroad, we would soon find the land a
place of shivering creatures, without the

capacity to live or the courage to die—
a calamity, surely. All these circumstances make for the hour of depression;
and it may well be in such an hour, amid
apathy and treachery, cold friends and
active enemies, with worn-down frame
and baffled mind, you, pleading for the
Old Cause, may feel your voice is indeed
a voice crying in the wilderness; and it
may serve till the blood warms again and
the imagination recover its glow, to think
how a Voice, that cried in the wilderness
thousands of years ago, is potent and inspiring now, where the voice of the
"practical" man sends no whisper across
the waste of years.

XI

What, then, to conclude, must be our
decision? To take our philosophy into
life. When we do that generally, in a deep
and significant sense our War of Independence will have begun. Let there be no
deferring a duty to a more convenient
future. It is as possible that an opening
for freedom may be thrust on us, as
that we shall be required to organise a
formal war with the usual movements of
armies; in our assumptions for the second,
let us not be guilty of the fatal error of

overlooking the first. As in other spheres, so in politics we have our conventions; and how little they may be proven has been lately seen, when England went through a war of debate,* largely unreal, over her constitution and her liberties, even while foreign wars and complications were still being debated; and in the middle of it all, suddenly, from a local labour dispute, putting by all thought of the constitution, feeling as comparatively insignificant the fear of invasion, all England stood shuddering on the verge of frantic civil war;† and all Ireland, when the moment of possible freedom was given, when England might have been hardly able to save herself, much less to hold us—Ireland, thinking and working in old grooves, lay helpless. Let us draw the moral. We cannot tell what unsuspected development may spring on us from the future, but we can always be prepared by understanding that the vital hour is the hour at hand. Let the brave choice now be made, and let the life around be governed by it; let every man stand to his colours and strike his flag to none; then shall we recover ground in all direc-

* Debate over House of Lords.
† The Railway strike.

tions, and our time shall be recorded, not with the deadening but with the luminous years. In all the vicissitudes of the fight, let us not be distracted by the meanness of the mere time-server nor the treachery of the enemy, but be collected and cool; and remembering the many who are not with us from honest motives or unsuspected fears, live to show our belief beautiful and true and, in the eternal sense, practical. Then shall those who are worth convincing be held, and our difference may reduce itself to what is possible; then will they come to realise that he who maintains a great faith unshaken will make more things possible than the opportunist of the hour; then will they understand how much more is possible than they had ever dared to dream : they will have a vision of the goal; and with that vision will be born a steady enthusiasm, a clear purpose, and a resolute soul. The regeneration of the land will be no longer a distant dream but a shaping reality; the living flame will sweep through all hearts again; and Ireland will enter her last battle for freedom to emerge and reassume her place among the nations of the earth.

CHAPTER VII

LOYALTY

I

TO be loyal to his cause is the finest tribute that can be paid to any man. And since loyalty to the Irish cause has been the great virtue of Irishmen through all history, it is time to have some clear thinking as to who are the Irish rebels and who the true men. When a stupid Government, grasping our reverence for fidelity, tried to ban our heroes by calling them felons, it was natural we should rejoin by writing " The Felons of our Land " and heap ridicule on their purpose. But once this end was achieved we should have reverted to the normal attitude and written up as the true Irish Loyalists, Brian the Great, and Shane the Proud, the

valiant Owen Roe and the peerless Tone,
Mitchel and Davis—irreconcilables all.
When men revolt against an established
evil it is their loyalty to the outraged truth
we honour. We do not extol a rebel who
rebels for rebellion's sake. Let us be clear
on this point, or when we shall have re-
established our freedom after centuries of
effort it shall be open to every knave and
traitor to challenge our independence and
plot to readmit the enemy. Loyalty is the
fine attribute of the fine nature; the word
has been misused and maligned in Ireland : let us restore it to its rightful honour
by remembering it to be the virtue of our
heroes of all time. In considering it from
this view-point we shall find occasion to
touch on delicate positions that have often
baffled and worried us—the asserting of
our rights while using the machinery of
the Government that denies them, the
burning question of consistency, our attitude towards the political adventurer on
one hand, and towards the honest man of
half-measures on the other. Loyalty involves all this. And it shows that the
man who revolts to win freedom is the
same as he who dies to defend it. He does
not change his face and nature with the

changing times. He is loyal always and most wonderfully lovable, because in the darkest times, when banned as wild, wicked and rebelly, he is loyal still as from the beginning, and will be to the end. Yes, Tone is the true Irish Loyalist, and every aider and abettor of the enemy a rebel to Ireland and the Irish race.

II

When you insist on examining the question in the light of first principles your opportunist opponent at once feels the weakness of his position and always turns the point on your consistency. It is well, then, in advance to understand the relative value and importance of argument as argument in the statement of any case. A body of principles is primarily of value, not as affording a case that can be argued with ingenuity, but as enshrining one great principle that shines through and informs the rest, that illumines the mind of the individual, that warms, clarifies and invigorates—that, so to speak, puts the mind in focus, gets the facts of existence into perspective, and gives the individual everything in its right place and true proportion. It brings a man to

H

the point where he does not dispute but believes. He has been wandering about cold and irresolute, tasting all philosophies, or none, and drinking deep despair. He does not understand the want in his soul while he has been looking for some panacea for its cure till the great light streams on him, and instead of receiving something he finds himself. That is it. There is a power of vision latent in us, clouded by error; the true philosophy dissipates the cloud and leaves the vision clear, wonderful and inspiring. He who acquired that vision is impervious to argument—it is not that he despises argument; on the contrary, he always uses it to its full strength. But he has had awakened within him something which the mere logician can never deduce, and that mysterious something is the explanation of his transformed life. He was a doubter, a falterer, a failure; he has become a believer, a fighter, a conqueror. You miss his significance completely when you take him for a theorist. The theorist propounds a view to which he must convert the world; the philosopher has a rule of life to immediately put into practice. His spirit flashes with a swiftness that can

be encircled by no theory.   It is his glory to
have over and above a new penetrating argument in the mind—a new and wonderful
vitality in the blood.   The unbeliever,
near by, still muddled by his cold theories,
will argue and debate till his intellect is
in a tangle. He fails to see that a man of
intellectual agility might frame a theory
and argue it out ably, and then suddenly
turn over and with equal dexterity argue
the other side. Do we not have set debates
with speakers appointed on each side?
That is dialectic—a trick of the mind.
But philosophy is the wine of the spirit.
The capacity then to argue the point is not
the justification of a philosophy.   That
justification must be found in the virtue
of the philosophy that gives its believer
vision and grasp of life as a whole, that
warms and quickens his heart and makes
him in spirit buoyant, beautiful, wise and
daring.

III

Let us come now to that burning ques-
tion of consistency.   "Very well, you
won't acknowledge the English Crown.
Why then use English coins and stamps?
You don't recognise the Parliament at
Westminster. Why then recognise the

County Councils created by Bill at Westminster? Why avail of all the Local Government machinery?"—and so forth. The argument is a familiar one, and the answer is simple. Though no guns are thundering now, Ireland is virtually in a state of war. We are fighting to recover independence. The enemy has had to relax somewhat in the exigencies of the struggle and to concede all these positions of local government and enterprise now in question. We take these posts as places conceded in the fight and avail of them to strengthen, develop and uplift the country and prepare her to carry the last post. Surely this is adequate. On a field of battle it is always to the credit of a general to capture an enemy's post and use it for the final victory. It is a sign of the battle's progress, and tells the distant watchers on the hills how the fight is faring and who is going to win. There would be consternation away from the field only if word should come that the soldiers had gone into the tents of the enemy, acknowledging him and accepting his flag. That is the point to question. There can be no defence for the occupying of any post conceded by the enemy. It may be held for or against Ireland; any man accepting it and surrendering his flag to hold it stands condemned thereby. That is clear. Yet it may be objected that such a clear choice is not put to most of those undertaking the local government of Ireland, that few are conscious of such an issue and few governed by it. It is true. But for all that the machinery of local government is clearly under popular control, and as clearly worked for an immediate good, preparing for a greater end. Men unaware of it are unconsciously working for the general development of the country and recovering her old power and influence. Those conscious of the deeper issue enter every position to further that development and make the end obvious when the alien Government— finding those powers conceded to sap further resistance are on the contrary used to conquer wider fields—endeavours to force the popular government back to the purposes of an old and failing tyranny. That is the nature of the struggle now. At periods the enemy tries to stem the movement, and then the fight becomes general and keen around a certain position. In our time there were the Land

Leagues, the Land War, fights for Home
Rule, Universities, Irish; and these fights
ended in Land Acts, Local Government
Acts, University Acts, and the conceding
of pride of place to the native language in
university life. Every position gained
is a step forward; it is accepted as such,
and so is justified. For anyone who grasps
the serious purpose of recovering Ireland's independence all along the line, the
suggestion that we should abandon all
machinery of local government and enterprise—because they are " Government
positions "—to men definitely attached to
the alien garrison is so foolish as not to be
even entertained. When our attitude is
questioned let it be made clear. That is
the final answer to the man who chal-
lenges our consistency : we are carrying
the trenches of the enemy.

IV

Even while dismissing a false idea of
consistency we have to make clear another
view still remote from the general mind.
If we are to have an effective army of freedom we must enrol only men who have a
clear conception of the goal, a readiness to
yield full allegiance, and a determination

to fight always so as to reflect honour on the flag. The importance of this will be felt only when we come to deal with concrete cases. While human nature is what it is we will have always on the outskirts of every movement a certain type of political adventurer who is ready to transfer his allegiance from one party to another according as he thinks the time serves. He has no principle but to be always with the ascendant party, and to succeed in that aim he is ready to court and betray every party in turn. As a result, he is a character well known to all. The honest man who has been following the wrong path, and after earnest inquiry comes to the flag, we readily distinguish. But it is fatal to any enterprise where the adventurer is enlisted and where his influence is allowed to dominate. It may seem strange that such men are given entry to great movements : the explanation is found in the desire of pioneers to make converts at once and convince the unconverted by the confidence of growing numbers. We ignore the danger to our growing strength when the adventurer comes along, loud in protest of his support—he is always affable and plausible, and is received as a

"man of experience"; and in our anxiety
for further strength we are apt to admit
him without reserve. But we must make
sure of our man. We must keep in mind
that an alliance with the adventurer is
more dangerous than his opposition; and
we must remember the general public, typi-
fied by the man in the street whom we
wish to convince, is quietly studying us,
attracted perhaps by our principles and
coming nearer to examine. If he knows
nothing else, he knows the unprincipled
man, and when he sees such in our ranks
and councils he will not wait to argue or
ask questions; he will go away and remain
away. The extent to which men are ruled
by the old adage, " Show me your company and I'll tell you what you are," is
more widespread than we think. More-
over, consistency in a fine sense is
involved in our decision. We fight for
freedom, not for the hope of material profit
or comfort, but because every fine instinct
of manhood demands that man be free,
and life beautiful and brave, and surely
in such a splendid battle to have as allies
mean, crafty profit-seekers would be
amazing. Let us be loyal in the deep
sense, and let us not be afraid of being

few at first. An earnest band is more
effective than a discreditable multitude.
That band will increase in numbers and
strength till it becomes the nucleus of an
army that will be invincible.

V

The fine sense of consistency that keeps
us clear of the adventurer decides also our
attitude to the well-meaning man of half-
measures. He says separation from England is not possible now and suggests
some alternative, if not Home Rule, Grat-
tan's Parliament, or leaving it an open
question. In the general view this seems
sensible, and we are tempted to make an
alliance based on such a ground; and the
alliance is made. What ensues? Men
come together who believe in complete
freedom, others who believe in partial
freedom that may lead to complete freedom, and others who are satisfied with
partial freedom as an end. Before long
the alliance ends in a deadlock. The man
of the most far-reaching view knows that
every immediate action taken must be
consistent with the wider view and the
farther goal, if that goal is to be attained;
and he finds that his ultimate principle

is frequently involved in some action proposed for the moment. When such a
moment comes he must be loyal to his flag
and to a principle that if not generally
acknowledged is an abiding rule with
him; but his allies refuse to be bound by
a principle that is an unwritten law for
him because the law is not written down
for them. This is the root of the trouble.
The friends, thinking to work together for
some common purpose, find the unsettled
issue intrudes, and a debate ensues that
leads to angry words, recriminations, bad
feeling and disruption. The alliance based
on half measures has not fulfilled its own
purpose, but it has sown suspicion between the honest men whom it brought
together; that is no good result from the
practical proposal. There is an inference :
men who are conscious of a clear complete
demand should form their own plans,
equally full of care and resolution, and
go ahead on their own account. But we
hear a plaintive cry abroad : " Oh, another
split; that's Irishmen all over—can never
unite," etc. We will not turn aside for the
plaintive people; but let it be understood there can be an independent co-
operation, where of use, with those honest

men who will not go the whole way. That independent co-operation can serve the full purpose of the binding alliance that has proved fatal. Above all, let there be no charge of bad faith against the earnest man who chooses other ways than ours; it is altogether indefensible because we disagree with him to call his motives in question. Often he is as earnest as we are; often has given longer and greater service, and only qualifies his own attitude in anxiety to meet others. To this we cannot assent, but to charge him with bad faith is flagrantly unjust and always calamitous. In getting rid of the deadlock we have too often fallen to furiously fighting with one another. Let us bear this in mind, and concern ourselves more with the common enemy; but let not the hands of the men in the vanguard be tied by alien King, Constitution, or Parliament. All the conditions grow more definite and seem, perhaps, too exacting; remember the greatness of the enterprise. Suppose in the building of a mighty edifice the architect at any point were careless or slurred over a difficulty, trusting to luck to bring it right, how the whole building would go awry, and what a mighty collapse would

follow. Let us stick to our colours and
have no fear. When all these principles
have been combined into one consistent
whole, a light will flash over the land and
the old spirit will be reborn; the mean
will be purged of their meanness, the timid
heartened with a fine courage, and the
fearless will be justified : the land will be
awake, militant, and marching to victory.

VI

This is, surely, the fine view of loyalty.
Let us write it on our banners and proclaim it to the world.   It is consistent,
honourable,   fearless   and   immutable.
What   is   said   here   to-day   with   enthusiasm, exactness and care, will stand
without emendation or enlargement, if in
a temporary reverse we are called to stand
in the dock to-morrow; or if, finely purged
in the battle of freedom, we come through
our last fight with splendid triumph, our
loyalty is there still, shining like a great
sun, the same beautiful, unchanging thing
that has lighted us through every struggle
—perhaps now to guide us in framing a
constitution and giving to a world, distracted by kings, presidents and theorists,
a new polity for nations. A waverer, half-

caught between the light, half fearful with an old fear, pleads : " This is too much— we are men, not angels." Precisely, we are not angels; and because of our human weakness, our erring minds, our sudden passions, the most confident of us may at any moment find himself in the mud. What, then, will uplift him if he has been a waverer in principle as well as in fact? He is helpless, disgraced and undone. Let him know in time we do not set up fine principles in a fine conceit that we can easily live up to them, but in the full consciousness that we cannot possibly live away from them. That is the bed-rock truth. When the man of finer faith by any slip comes to the earth, he has to uplift him a staff that never fails, and to guide him a principle that strengthens him for another fight, to go forth, in a sense Alexander never dreamed of, to conquer new worlds. 'Tis the faith that is in him, and the flag he serves, that make a man worthy; and the meanest may be with the highest if he be true and give good service. Let us put by then the broken reed and the craft of little minds, and give us for our saving hope the banner of the angels and the loyalty of gods and men.

CHAPTER VIII

WOMANHOOD

" And another said : I have married a wife and therefore I cannot come."

Y ES, and we have been satisfied always to blame the wife, without noticing the man who is fond of his comfort first of all, who slips quietly away to enjoy a quiet smoke and a quiet glass in some quiet nook—always securing his escape by the readiest excuse. We are coming now to consider the aspect of the question that touches our sincere manhood; but let no one think we overlook that mean type of man who evades every call to duty on the comfortable plea : "I have married a wife."

I

When the mere man approaches the woman to study her, we can imagine the

fair ones getting together and nudging
one another in keen amusement as to
what this seer is going to say. It is often
sufficiently amusing when the clumsy
male approaches her with self-satisfied
air, thinking he has the secret of her
mysterious being. I have no intention
here of entering a rival search for the
secret. But we can, perhaps, startle the
gay ones from merriment to gravity by
stating the simple fact that every man
stands in some relationship to woman,
either as son, brother, or husband; and if
it be admitted that there is to be a fight
to-morrow, then there are some things to
be settled to-day. How is the woman
training for to-morrow? How, then, will
the man stand by that very binding relationship? Will clinging arms hold him
back or proud ones wave him on? Will he
have, in place of a comrade in the fight,
a burden; or will the battle that has too
often separated them but give them closer
bonds of union and more intimate knowledge of the wonderful thing that is Life?

II

I wish to concentrate on one heroic
example of Irish Womanhood that should

serve as a model to this generation; and I do not mean to dwell on much that would require detailed examination. But some points should be indicated. For example, the awakening consciousness of our womanhood is troubling itself rightly over the woman's place in the community, is concentrating on the type delineated in "The Doll's House," and is agitating for a more honourable and dignified place. We applaud the pioneers thus fighting for their honour and dignity : but let them not make the mistake of assuming the men are wholly responsible for "The Doll's House," and the women would come out if they could. We have noticed the man who prefers his ease to any troubling duty : he has his mate in the woman who prefers to be wooed with trinkets, chocolates, and the theatre to a more beautiful way of life, that would give her a nobler place but more strenuous conditions. Again, the man is not always the lord of the house. He is as often, if not more frequently, its slave. Then there are the conventions of life. In place of a fine sense of courtesy prevailing between man and woman, which would recognise with the woman's finer sensibility a fine self-reliance, and with the man's greater strength a fine gentleness, we have a false code of manners, by which the woman is to be taken about, petted and treated generally as the useless being she often is; while the man becomes an effeminate creature that but cumbers the earth. Fine courtesy and fine comradeship go together. But we have allowed a standard to gain recognition that is a danger alike to the dignity of our womanhood and the virility of our manhood. It is for us who are men to labour for a finer spirit in our manhood : we cannot throw the blame for any weakness over on external conditions. The woman is in the same position. She must understand that greater than the need of the suffrage is the more urgent need of making her fellow-woman spirited and self-reliant, ready rather to anticipate a danger than to evade it. When she is thus trained, not all the men of all the nations can deny her recognition and equality.

III

For the battle of to-morrow then there is a preliminary fight to-day. The woman must come to this point, too. In life there is frequently so much meanness, a man is

I

often called to acknowledge some degrading standard or fight for the very recognition of manhood, and the woman must stand in with him or help to pull him down. Let her understand this and her duty is present and urgent. The man so often wavers on the verge of the right path, the woman often decides him. If she is nobler than he, as is frequently the case, she can lift him to her level; if she is meaner, as she often is, she as surely drags him down. When they are both equal in spirit and nobility of nature, how the world is filled with a glory that should assure us, if nothing else could, of the truth of the Almighty God and a beautiful Eternity to explain the origin and destiny of their wonderful existence. They are indispensable to each other : if they stand apart, neither can realise in its fulness the beauty and glory of life. Let the man and woman see this, and let them know in the day that is at hand, how the challenge may come from some petty authority of the time that rules not by its integrity but by its favourites. We are cursed with such authority, and many a one drives about in luxury because he is obsequious to it : he prefers to be a parasite and to live in splendour than be a man and live in straits. He has what Bernard Shaw so aptly calls "the soul of a servant." If we are to prepare for a braver future, let us fight this evil thing; if we are to put by national servitude, let us begin by driving out individual obsequiousness. This is our training ground for to-morrow. Let the woman realise this, and at least as many women as men will prefer privation with self-respect to comfort with contempt. Let us, then, in the name of our common nature, ask those who have her training in hand, to teach the woman to despise the man of menial soul and to loathe the luxury that is his price.

IV

I wish to come to the heroic type of Irish Womanhood. When we need to hearten ourselves or others for a great enterprise, we instinctively turn to the examples of heroes and heroines who, in similar difficulties to ours, have entered the fight bravely, and issued heroically, leaving us a splendid heritage of fidelity and achievement. It is little to our credit that our heroes are so little known. It is less to our credit that our heroines are

hardly known at all; and when we praise
or sing of one our selection is not always
the happiest. How often in the concert-
hall or drawing-room do we get emotional
when someone sings in tremulous tones,
" She is far from the Land." There is a feeling for poetry in our lives, a feeling that
patriotism will not have it, a melting pity
for the love that went to wreck, a sympathy for ourselves and everybody and
everything—a relaxing of all the nerves
in a wave of sentiment. This emotion is
of the enervating order. There is no
sweep of strong fire through the blood, no
tightening grip on life, no set resolve
to stand to the flag and see the battle
through. It is well, then, a generation
that has heard from a thousand plat-
forms, in plaintive notes, of Sarah Curran
and her love should turn to the braver
and more beautiful model of her who was
the wife of Tone.

v

When we think of the qualities that are
distinctive of the woman, we have in
mind a finer gentleness, sensibility, sympathy and tenderness; and when we have
these qualities intensified in any woman,

and with them combined the endurance,
courage and daring that are taken as the
manly virtues, we have a woman of the
heroic type. Of such a type was the wife
of Tone. We can speak her praise without fear, for she was put to the test in
every way, and in every way found marvellously true. For her devotion to, and
encouragement of, her great husband in
his great work, she would have won our
high praise, even if, when he was stricken
down and she was bereft of his wonderful love and buoyant spirits, she had
proved forgetful of his work and the glory
of his name. But she was bereft, and she
was then found most marvellously true.
Her devotion to Tone, while he was living and fighting, might be explained by
the woman's passionate attachment to the
man she loved. It is the woman's tenderness that is most evident in these early
years, but there is shining evidence of the
fortitude that showed her true nobility in
the darker after-years. It was no ordinary love that bound them, and reading
the record of their lives this stands out
clear and beautiful. Tone, whom we
know as patient organiser, tenacious
fighter, far-seeing thinker, indomitable

spirit—a born leader of men—writes to his wife with the passionate simplicity of an enraptured child : " I doat upon you and the babes." And his letters end thus : " Kiss the babies for me ten thousand times. God Almighty for ever bless you, my dearest life and soul." (This from the " French Atheist." I hope his traducers are heartily ashamed of themselves.) Nor is it strange. When, in the beginning of his enterprise, he is in America, preparing to go to France on his great mission, he is troubled by the thought of his defenceless ones. In the crisis how does his wife act? Does she wind clinging arms around him, telling him with tears, of their children and his early vows, and beseeching him to think of his love and forget his country? No; let the diary speak : " My wife especially, whose courage and whose zeal for my honour and interests were not in the least abated by all her past sufferings, supplicated me to let no consideration of her or our children stand for a moment in the way of my engagements to our friends and my duty to my country, adding that she would answer for our family during my absence, and that the same Providence which had so often, as it were, miraculously preserved us, would, she was confident, not desert us now." It is the unmistakable accent of the woman. She is quivering as she sends him forth, but the spirit in her eyes would put a trembling man to shame—a spirit that her peerless husband matched but no man could surpass. Her fortitude was to be more terribly tried in the terrible after-time, when the Cause went down in disaster and Tone had to answer with his life. No tribute could be so eloquent as the letter he wrote to her when the last moment had come and his doom was pronounced: "Adieu, dearest love, I find it impossible to finish this letter. Give my love to Mary; and, above all, remember you are now the only parent of our dearest children, and that the best proof you can give of your affection for me will be to preserve yourself for their education. God Almighty bless you all." That letter is like Stephens' speech from the dock, eloquent for what is left unsaid. There is no wailing for her, least of all for himself, not that their devoted souls were not on the rack: "As no words can express what I feel for you and our children, I shall not attempt it; complaint of any kind would be beneath your courage and mine "—but their souls, that were destined to suffer, came sublimely through the ordeal. When Tone left his children as a trust to his wife, he knew from the intimacy of their union what we learn from the after-event, how that trust might be placed and how faithfully it would be fulfilled. What a tribute from man to wife! How that trust was fulfilled is in evidence in every step of the following years. Remembering Tone's son who survived to write the memoirs was a child at his father's death, his simple tribute written in manhood is eloquent in the extreme : " I was brought up by my surviving parent in all the principles and in all the feelings of my father "—of itself it would suffice. But we can follow the years between and find moving evidence of the fulfilment of the trust. We see her devotion to her children and her proud care to preserve their independence and her own. She puts by patronage, having a higher title as the widow of a General of France; and she wins the respect of the great ones of France under the Republic and the Empire. Lucien Buonaparte, a year after Tone's death, pleaded before the Council of Five Hundred, in warm and eloquent praise : "If the services of Tone were not sufficient of themselves to rouse your feelings, I might mention the independent spirit and firmness of that noble woman who, on the tomb of her husband and her brother, mingles with her sighs aspirations for the deliverance of Ireland. I would attempt to give you an expression of that Irish spirit which is blended in her countenance with the expression of her grief. Such were those women of Sparta, who, on the return of their countrymen from the battle, when with anxious looks they ran over the ranks and missed amongst them their sons, their husbands, and their brothers, exclaimed, 'He died for his country; he died for the Republic.'" When the Republic fell, and in the upheaval her rights were ignored, she went to the Emperor Napoleon in person and, recalling the services of Tone, sought naturalization for her son to secure his career in the army; and to the wonder of all near by, the Emperor heard her with marked respect and immediately granted her request. She sought only this for her surviving son. She had seen two children die—there was moving pathos in the daughter's death—

and now she was standing by the last. Never was child guarded more faithfully or sent more proudly on his path in life. One should read the memoirs to understand, and pause frequently to consider : how she promised her husband bravely in the beginning that she would answer for their children, and how, in what she afterwards styled the hyperbole of grief, she was called to fulfil to the letter, and was found faithful, with an unexampled strength and devotion; how she saw two children struck down by a fatal disease, and how she drew the surviving son back to health by her watchful care to send him on his college and military career with loving pride; how, when a Minister of France, irritated at her putting by his patronage, roughly told her he could not " take the Emperor by the collar to place Mr. Tone "—she went to the Emperor in person, with dignity but without fear, and won his respect; how the suggestion of the mean-minded that her demand was a pecuniary one, drew from her the proud boast that in all her misfortunes she had never learned to hold out her hand; how through all her misfortunes we watch her with wonderful dignity, delicacy, courage,

and devotion quick to see what her trust
demanded and never failing to answer the
call, till her task is done, and we see her
on the morning when her son sets out on
the path she had prepared, the same
quivering woman, who had sent her husband with words of comfort to his duty,
now, after all the years of trial, sending
her son as proudly on his path. It is their
first parting. Let her own words speak :
" Hitherto I had not allowed myself even
to feel that my William was my own and
my only child; I considered only that
Tone's son was confided to me; but in that
moment Nature resumed her rights. I sat
in a field : the road was long and white
before me and no object on it but my child.
.   .   .   . I could not think; but all I had
ever suffered seemed before and around
me at that moment, and I wished so in-
tensely to close my eyes for ever, that I
wondered it did not happen. The transitions
of the mind are very extraordinary. As I
sat in that state, unable to think of the
necessity of returning home, a little lark
rushed up from the grass beside me; it
whirled over my head and hovered in the
air singing such a beautiful, cheering,
and, as it sounded to me, approving note,

that it roused me. I felt in my heart as if Tone had sent it to me. I returned to my solitary home." It is a picture to move us, to think of the devoted woman there in the sunshine, bent down in the grass, utterly alone, till the lark, sweeping heavenward in song, seems to give a message of gentle comfort from her husband's watching spirit. Our emotion now is of no enervating order. We are proud of our land and her people; our nerves are firm and set; our hearts cry out for action; we are not weeping, but burning for the Cause. How little we know of this heroic woman. We are in some ways familiar with Tone, his high character, his genial open nature, his daring, his patience, his farsightedness, his judgment—in spirit tireless and indomitable : a man peerless among his fellows. But he had yet one compeer; there was one nature that matched his to depth and height of its greatness—that nature was a woman's, and the woman was Wolfe Tone's wife.

VI

It is well this heroic example of our womanhood should be before not only our womanhood but our manhood. It should show us all that patriotism does not destroy the finer feelings, but rather calls them forth and gives them wider play. We have been too used to thinking that the qualities of love and tenderness are no virtues for a soldier, that they will sap his resolution and destroy his work; but our movements fail always when they fail to be human. Until we mature and the poetry in life is wakening, we are ready to act by a theory; but when Nature asserts herself the hard theorist fails to hold us. Let us remember and be human. We have been saying in effect, if not in so many words : "For Ireland's sake, don't fall in love"—we might as well say : "For Ireland's sake, don't let your blood circulate." It is impossible—even if it were possible it would be hateful. The man and woman have a great and beautiful destiny to fulfil together : to substitute for it an unnatural way of life that can claim neither the seclusion of the cloister nor the dominion of the world is neither beautiful nor great. We have cause for gratitude in the example before us. The woman can learn from it how she may equal the bravest man; and the man should learn to let his wife and children suffer rather than make of them willing slaves and cowards. For there are some earnest men who are ready to suffer themselves but cannot endure the suffering of those they love, and a mistaken family tenderness binds and drags them down. No one, surely, can hold it better to carefully put away every duty that may entail hardship on wife and child, for then the wife is, instead of a comrade, a burden, and the child becomes a degenerate creature, creeping between heaven and earth, afraid to hold his head erect, and unable to fulfil his duty to God or man. Let no man be afraid that those he loves may be tried in the fire; but let him, to the best of his strength, show them how to stand the ordeal, and then trust to the greatness of the Truth and the virtue of a loyal nature to bring each one forth in triumph, and he and they may have in the issue undreamed of recompense. For the battle that tries them will discover finer chords not yet touched in their intercourse; finer sympathies, susceptibilities, gentleness and strength; a deeper insight into life and a wider outlook on the world, making in fine a wonderful blend of wisdom, tenderness and courage that gives them to realise that life, with all its faults, struggles, and pain is still and for ever great and beautiful.

CHAPTER IX

THE FRONTIER

I

OUR frontier is twofold, the language and the sea. For the majesty of our encircling waters we have no need to raise a plea, but to give God thanks for setting so certain a seal on our individual existence and giving us in the spreading horizon of the ocean some symbol of our illimitable destiny. For the language there is something still to be said; there are some ideas gaining currency that should be challenged—the cold denial of some that the unqualified name Irish be given to the literature of Irishman that is passionate with Irish enthusiasm and loyalty to Ireland, yet from the exigencies of the time had to be written in English; the view not

only assumed but asserted by some of the
Gael that the Gall may be recognised only
if he take second place; the aloofness of
many of the Gall, not troubling to understand their rights and duties; the ignoring
on both sides of the fine significance of the
name Irishman, of a spirit of patriotism
and a deep-lying basis of authority and
justice that will give stability to the state
and secure its future against any upheaval
that from the unrest of the time would
seem to threaten the world.

II

Consider first the literature of Irishmen
in English. From the attitude commonly
taken on the question of literary values,
it is clear that the primary significance
of expression in writing is often lost. What
is said, and the purpose for which it is
said, take precedence of the medium
through which it is said. But from our
national awakening to the significance of
the medium so long ignored we have
grown so excited that we frequently forget
the greater significance of the thing. The
utterance of the man is of first importance,
and, where his utterance has weight, the
vital need is to secure it through some

medium, the medium becoming important when one more than another is found to have a wider and more intimate appeal; and then we do well to become insistent for a particular medium when it is in anxiety for full delivery of the writer's thought and a wide knowledge of its truth. But we are losing sight of this natural order of things. It is well, then, the un-convinced Gall should hear why he should accept the Irish language; not simply to defer to the Gael, but to quicken the mind and defend the territory of what is now the common country of the Gael and Gall. Davis caught up the great signi-ficance of the language when he said : "'Tis a surer barrier, and more important frontier, than fortress or river." The lan-guage is at once our frontier and our first fortress, and behind it all Irishmen should stand, not because a particular branch of our people evolved it, but because it is the common heritage of all. One who has a knowledge of Irish can easily get evidence of its quickening power on the Irish mind. Travel in an Irish-speaking district and hail one of its old people in English, and you get in response a dull "Good-day, Sir." Salute him in Irish and you touch

K

a secret spring. The dull eyes light up, the face is all animation, the body alert, and for a dull "good-day," you get warm benedictions, lively sallies, and after you, as you pass on your road, a flood of rich and racy Irish comes pouring down the wind. That is the secret power of the language. It makes the old men proud of their youth and gives to the young quickened faculties, an awakened imagination and a world to conquer. This is no exaggeration. It is not always obvious, because we do not touch the secret spring nor wander near the magic. But the truth is there to find for him who cares to search. You discover behind the dullness of a provincial town a bright centre of interest, and when you study the circle you know that here is some wonderful thing : priests, doctors, lawyers, teachers, tradesmen, clerks—all drawn together, young and old, both sexes, all enthusiasts. Sometimes a priest is teaching a smith, sometimes the smith is teaching the priest : for a moment at least we have unconsciously levelled barriers and there is jubilation in the natural life re-born. Out of that quickened life and consciousness rises a vivid imagination with a rush of thought and a power of expression that gives the nation a new literature. That is the justification of the language. It awakens and draws to expression minds that would otherwise be blank. It is not that the revelation of Davis is of less value than we think, but that through the medium of Irish other revelations will be won that would otherwise be lost. Again, in subtle ways we cannot wholly understand, it gives the Irish mind a defence against every other mind, taking in comradeship whatever good the others have to offer, while retaining its own power and place. The Irish mind can do itself justice only in Irish. But still some ardent and faithful spirits broke through every difficulty of time and circumstance and found expression in English, and we have the treasures of Davis, Mitchel, and Mangan; yet, the majority remained cold, and now, to quicken the mass, we turn to the old language. But this is not to decry what was won in other fields. In the widening future that beckons to us, we shall, if anything, give greater praise to these good fighters and enthusiasts, who in darker years, even with the language of the enemy, resisted his march and held the gap for Ireland.

III

On this ground the Gael and Gall stand
on footing of equality. That is the point
many on both sides miss and we need to
emphasise it. Some Irishmen not of Gaelic
stock speak of Irish as foreign to them, and
would maintain English in the principal
place now and in the future. We do well
then to make clear to such a one that he is
asked to adopt the language for Ireland's
sake as a nation and for his own sake as a
citizen. If he wishes to serve her he must
stand for the language; if he prefers English civilisation he should go back to England. There only can he develop on
English lines. An Irishman in Ireland
with an English mind is a queer contradic-
tion, who can serve neither Ireland nor
England in any good sense, and both Ireland and England disown him. So the
Irishman of other than Gaelic ancestors
should stand in with us, not accepting
something disagreeable as inevitable, but
claiming a right by birth and citizenship,
joining the fine army of the nation for a
brave adventurous future, full of fine pos-
sibility and guaranteed by a fine comrade-

ship—owning a land not of flattery and favouritism, but of freedom and manhood. This saving ideal has been often obscured by our sundering class names. This is why we would substitute as common for all the fine name of Irishman.

IV

But in asking all parties to accept the common name of Irishman, we find a fear rather suggested than declared—that men may be asked in this name to put by something they hold as a great principle of Life; that Catholic, Protestant and Dissenter will all be asked to find agreement in a fourth alternative, in which they will not submit to one another but will all equally belie themselves. There is such a hidden fear, and we should have it out and dispose of it. The best men of all parties will have no truck with this and they are right. But on what ground, then, shall we find agreement, the recognition of which Irish Citizenship implies? On this, that the man of whatever sincere principles, religious or civic, counts among his great duties his duty as citizen; and he defends his creed because he believes it to be a safe guide to the fulfilling of all duties, this

including. When, therefore, we ask him
to stand in as Irish Citizen, it is not that
he is to abandon in one iota his sincere
principles, but that he is to give us proof
of his sincerity. He tells us his creed requires him to be a good citizen : we give
him a fine field in which he can be to us a
fine example.

v

In further consideration of this we
should put by the thought of finding a
mere working agreement. There is a deep-
lying basis of authority and justice to
seek, which it should be our highest aim
to discover. Modern governments concede justice to those who can compel
justice—even the democracy requires that
you be strong enough to formulate a claim
and sustain it; but this is the way of
tyranny. A perfect government should
seek, while careful to develop its stronger
forces and keep them in perfect balance,
to consider also the claims of those less
powerful but not less true. A government
that over-rides the weak because it is safe,
is a tyranny, and tyranny is in seed in the
democratic governments of our time. We
must consider this well, for it is pressing

and grave; and we must get men to come
together as citizens to defend the rights as
well of the unit which is unsupported as
of the party that commands great power.
So shall we give steadiness and fervour to
our growing strength by balancing it with
truth and justice : so shall we found a
government that excesses cannot under-
mine nor tyranny destroy.

VI

We have to consider, in conclusion, the
unrest in the world, the war of parties and
classes, and the need of judging the tendencies of the time to set our steps aright.
With the wars and rumours of wars that
threaten the great nations from without
and the wild upheavals that threaten them
within, it would be foolish to hide from
ourselves the drift of events. We must
decide our attitude; and if it is too much
to hope that we may keep clear of the upheavals, we should aim at strengthening
ourselves against the coming crash. We
cannot set the world right, but we can go
a long way to setting things in our own
land right, by making through a common
patriotism a united people. What if we
are held up occasionally by the cold cries

shot at every high aim—"dreamer—
Utopia "; cry this in return : no vision of
the dreamer can be more wild than the
frantic make-shifts of the Great Powers to
vie in armaments with one another or re-
press internal revolts. Consider England
in the late strike that paralysed her.   It
was only suspended by a step that merely
deferred the struggle; the strife is again
threatening.   All the powers are so
threatened and their efforts to defer the
hour are equally feverish and fruitless; for
the hour is pressing and may flash on the
world when 'tis least prepared.   Let who
will deride us, but let us prepare.   We may
not guide our steps with the certainty of
prophets, nor hope by our beautiful
schemes to make a perfect state; but we
can only come near to perfection in the
light of a perfect ideal, and however far
below it we may remain, we can at least,
under its inspiration, reach an existence
rational and human : our justification for
a brave effort lies in that the governments
of this time are neither one nor the other.
He who thinks Ireland's struggle to express her own mind, to give utterance to
her own tongue, to stand behind her own
frontier, is but a sentiment will be sur-

prised to find it leads him to this point. Herein is the justification and the strength of the movement. Men are deriding things around them, of the significance of which they have not the remotest idea. Ireland is calling her children to a common banner, to the defence of her frontier, to the building up of a national life, harmonious and beautiful—a conception of citizenship, from which a right is conceded, not because it can be compelled, but because it is just : to the foundation of a state that will by its defence of the least powerful prove all powerful, that will be strong because true, beautiful because free, full of the music of her olden speech and caught by the magic of her encircling sea.

CHAPTER X

LITERATURE AND FREEDOM—THE PROPAGANDIST PLAYWRIGHT

I

A NATION'S literature is an index to its mind. If the nation has its freedom to win, from its literature may we learn if it is passionately in earnest in the fight, or if it is half-hearted, or if it cares not at all. Whatever state prevails, passionate men can pour their passion through literature to the nation's soul and make it burn and move and fight. For this reason it is of transcendent importance to the Cause. Literature is the Shrine of Freedom, its fortress, its banner, its charter. In its great temple patriots worship; from it soldiers go forth, wave its challenge, and fight, and conquering, write the charter of their country. Its great power is contested by none; rather, all recognise it, and many and violent are the disputes as to its right use and purpose. I propose to consider two of the disputants —the propagandist playwright and the art-for-art's-sake artist, since they raise issues that are our concern. It is curious that two so violently opposed should be so nearly alike in error : they are both afraid of life. The propagandist is all for one side; the artist afraid of every side. The one lacks imagination; the other lacks heart; they are both wide of the truth. The service of the truth requires them to pursue one course; in their dispute they swerve from that course, one to right, one to left. Because they leave the path on opposite sides, they do not see how much alike is their error; but that they do both leave the path is my point, and it is well we should consider it. It would be difficult to deal with both sides at once; so I will consider the propagandist first. What I have to charge against him is that his work is insincere, that he is afraid to do justice to the other side, that he makes ridicule of our exemplars, that he helps to keep the *poseur* in being; and to conclude, that only by a saving sense of humour can we find our way back to the truth.

II

When we judge literature we do so by reference to the eternal truth, not by what the writer considers the present phase of truth; and if literature so tested is found guilty of suppression, evasion or misinterpretation, we call the work insincere, though the author may have written in perfect good faith. That is a necessary distinction to keep in mind. If you call a man's work insincere, the superficial critic will take it as calling the man himself insincere; but the two are distinct, and it needs to be emphasised, for sincere men are making these propagandist plays, of which the manifest and glaring untruth is working mischief to the national mind. A type of such a play is familiar enough in these days when we like to ridicule the West Briton. We are served up puppets representing the shoneen with a lisp set over against the patriot who says all the proper things suitable to the occasion. Now, such a play serves no good purpose, but it has a certain bad effect. It does not give a true interpretation of life; it enlightens no one; but it flatters the prejudices of people who profess things for which they have no zeal.

That is the root of the mischief. Many of
us will readily profess a principle for
which we will not as readily suffer, but
when the pinch comes and we are asked
to do service for the flag, we cover our un-
willingness by calling the man on the other
side names. Where such a spirit prevails
there can be no national awakening. If we
put a play before the people, it must be
with a hope of arresting attention, striking
their imagination, giving them a grip of
reality, and filling them with a joy in life.
Now, the propagandist play does none of
these things; it has neither joy nor
reality; its characters are puppets and
ridiculous; they are essentially cari-
catures. This is supposed to convert the
unbeliever; but the intelligent unbeliever
coming to it is either bored or irritated by
its extravagant absurdity, and if he admits
our sincerity, it is only at the expense of
our intelligence.

III

A propagandist play for a political end
is even more mischievous—at least lovers
of freedom have more cause for protest. It
makes our heroes ridiculous. No man of
imagination can stand these impossible

persons of the play who "walk on" eternally talking of Ireland. Our heroes were
men; these are *poseurs*. Get to understand Davis, Tone, or any of our great
ones, and you will find them human, gay,
and lovable. "Were you ever in love,
Davis?" asked one of his wondering ad-
mirers, and prompt and natural came the
reply: "I'm never out of it." We swear
by Tone for his manly virtues; we love
him because we say to ourselves: "What
a fine fellow for a holiday." A friend of
Mitchel's travelling with him once through
a storm, was astonished to find him suddenly burst out into a fine recitation,
which he delivered with fine effect. He
was joyous in spirit. For their buoyancy
we love them all, and because of it we
emulate them. We are influenced, not by
the man who always wants to preach a sermon at us, but by the one with whom we
go for a holiday. Our history-makers were
great, joyous men, of fine spirit, fine
imagination, fine sensibility, and fine
humour. They loved life; they loved their
fellow man; they loved all the beautiful,
brave things of earth. When you know
them you can picture them scaling high
mountains and singing from the summits,

or boating on fine rivers in the sunlight,
or walking about in the dawn, to the music
of Creation, evolving the philosophy of
revolutions and building beautiful worlds.
You get no hint of this from the absurd
propagandist play, yet this is what the
heart of man craves. When he does not
get it, he cannot explain what he wants;
but he knows what he does not want, and
he goes away and keeps his distance. The
play has missed fire, and the playwright
and his hero are ridiculous. Let us understand one thing : if we want to make men
dutiful we must make them joyous.

IV

It is because we must talk of grave
things that we must preserve our gaiety;
otherwise we could not preserve our
balance. By some freak of nature, the
average man strikes attitudes as readily
as the average boy whistles. We know how
the *poseur* works mischief to every cause,
and we can see the *poseur* on every side.
In politics, he has made the platform contemptible, which is a danger to the nation,
needing the right use of platform; in literature—well, we all know bourgeois, but
who has done justice to the artist who gets

on a platform to talk about the bourgeois?
—in religion, the *poseur* is more likely to
make agnostics than all the Rationalist
Press; and the agnostic *poseur* in turn is
very funny. Now all these are an afflic-
tion, a collection of absurdities of which
we must cure the nation. If we cannot
cure the nation of absurdity we cannot set
her free. Let it be our rule to combine
gaiety with gravity and we will acquire a
saving sense of proportion. Only the
solemn man is dull; the serious man has a
natural fund of gaiety : we need only be
natural to bring back joy to serious endeavour. Then we shall begin to move. Let
us remember a revolution will surely fail
when its leaders have no sense of humour.

v

But our humour will not be a saving
humour unless it is of high order. A great
humorist is as rare as a great poet or a
great philosopher. Though ours may not
be great we must keep it in the line of
greatness. Remember, great humour must
be made out of ourselves rather than out
of others. The fine humorist is delightfully
courteous; the commonplace wit, invariably insulting. We must keep two things in

mind, that in laughter at our own folly is the beginning of wisdom; and the keenest wit is pure fun, never coarse fun. We start a laugh at others by getting an infallible laugh at ourselves. The commonplace wit arranges incidents to make someone he dislikes ridiculous; his attitude is the attitude of the superior person. He is nearly always—often unintentionally—offensive; he repels the public sometimes in irritation, sometimes in amusement, for they often see point in his joke, but see a greater joke in him, and they are often laughing, not at his joke, but at himself. Let us for our salvation avoid the attitude of the superior person. Don't make sport of others—make it of yourself. Ridicule of your neighbour must be largely speculation; of the comedy in yourself there can be no doubt. When you get the essential humour out of yourself, you get the infallible touch, and you arrest and attract everyone. You are not the superior person. In effect, you slap your neighbour on the back and say, "We're all in the same boat; let us enjoy the joke"; and you find he will come to you with glistening eye. He may feel a little foolish at first—you are poking his ribs; but you cannot help it—

L

having given him the way to poke your own. By your merry honesty he knows you for a safe comrade, and he comes with relief and confidence—we like to talk about ourselves. He will be equally frank with yourself; you will tell one another secrets; you will reach the heart of man. That is what we need. We must get the heart-beat into literature. Then will it quiver and dance and weep and sing. Then we are in the line of greatness.

VI

It is because we need the truth that we object to the propagandist playwright. Only in a rare case does he avoid being partial; and when he is impartial he is cold and unconvincing. He gives us argument instead of emotion; but emotion is the language of the heart. He does not touch the heart; he tries to touch the mind : he is a pamphleteer and out of place. He fails, and his failure has damaged his cause, for it leaves us to feel that the cause is as cold as his play; but when the Cause is a great one it is always vital, warm and passionate. It is for the sake of the Cause we ask that a play be made by a sincere man-of-letters, who will give us not propagandist literature nor art-for-art's-sake, but the throbbing heart of man. The great dramatist will have the great qualities needed, sensibility, sympathy, insight, imagination, and courage. The special pleader and the *poseur* lack all these things, and they make themselves and their work foolish. Let us stand for the truth, not pruning it for the occasion. The man who is afraid to face life is not competent to lead anyone, to speak for anyone, or to interpret anything : he inspires no confidence. The one to rouse us must be passionate, and his passion will win us heart and soul. When from some terribly intense moment, he turns with a merry laugh, only the fool will take him as laughing at his cause; the general instinct will see him detecting an attitude, tripping it up, and making us all merry and natural again. In that moment we shall spring up astonished, enthusiastic, exultant—here is cne inspired; we shall enter a passionate brotherhood, no cold disputes now—the smouldering fire along the land shall quicken to a blaze, history shall be again in the making. We shall be caught in the living flame.

CHAPTER XI

LITERATURE AND FREEDOM—ART FOR ART'S SAKE

I

ART for art's sake has come to have a meaning which must be challenged, but yet it can be used in a sense that is both high and sacred. If a gifted writer take literature as a great vocation and determine to use his talents faithfully and well, without reference to fee or reward; if prosperity cannot seduce him to the misuse of his genius, then we give him our high praise. Let it still not be forgotten that the labourer is worthy of his hire. But if the hire is not forthcoming, and he knowing it, yet says in his heart, "The work must still be done"; and if he does it loyally and bravely, despite the present

152

coldness of the world, doing the good work for the love of the work and all beautiful things; and if with this meaning he take " art for art's sake " as his battle-cry, then we repeat it is used in a sense both high and sacred.

II

But there are artists abroad whose chief glory seems to be to deny that they have convictions—that is, convictions about the passionate things of life that rouse and move their generation. Now that they should not be special pleaders is an obvious duty, but unless they have a passionate feeling for the vital things that move men, heart and soul, they cannot interpret the heart and soul of passionate men, and their work must be for ever cold. When literature is not passionate it does not touch the spirit to lift and spread its wings and soar to finer air. That is the great want about all the clever books now being turned out—they often give us excitement; they never give us ecstasy. Then there is an obvious feeling of something lacking which men try to make up with art; and they produce work faultless in form and fastidious in phrase, but still it lacks the touch of fire that would lift it from common things to greatness.

III

If we are to apply art to great work we must distinguish art from artifice. We find the two well contrasted in Synge's "Riders to the Sea" and his "Playboy." The first was written straight from the heart. We feel Synge must have followed those people carrying the dead body, and touched to the quick by the *caoine*, passed the touch on to us, for in the lyric swell of the close we get the true emotion. Here alone is he in the line of greatness. This gripped his heart and he wrote out of himself. But in the other work of his it was otherwise. He has put his method on record : he listened through a chink in the floor, and wrote around other people. It is characteristic of the art of our time. Let it be called art if the critics will, but it is not life.

IV

No, it is not life. But there is so much talk just now of getting "down to fundamentals," of the poetry of the tramp "walking the world," and the rest of it,

that it would be well if we *did get* down
to fundamentals; and this is one thing fundamental—the tramp is a deserter from
life. He evades the troubled field where
great causes are fought; he shuns the battle
because of the wounds and the sacrifice;
he has no heart for high conflict and victory. Let him under the cover of darkness
but secure his share of the spoils and the
world may go to wreck. Yes, he is the
meanest of things—a deserter. On the
field of battle he would be shot. If we let
him desert the field of life, go his way and
walk the world, let us not at least hail him
as a hero.

v

The Repertory Theatre is the nursery of
this particular art-cult, and 'twould relieve
some of us to talk freely about it. The
Repertory Theatre has already become
fashionable, and is quite rapidly become a
nuisance. Men are making songs and
plays and lectures for art's sake, for the
praise of a coterie or to shock the bourgeois
—above all shock the bourgeois. A certain
type of artist delights in shocking the
bourgeois—a riot over a play gives him
great satisfaction. In passing, one must

note with exasperation, perhaps with some
misgiving, how men raise a riot over something not worth a thought, and will not
fight for things for which they ought to
die. But he likes the bourgeois to think
him a terrible person; in his own esteem
he is on an eminence, and he proceeds to
send out more shock-the-bourgeois literature; and 'tis mostly very sorry stuff.
Sometimes he tries to be emotional and is
but painfully artificial; sometimes he tries
to be merry and gives us flippancy for fun.
And we feel a terrible need for getting back
to a standard, worthy and true. Great
work can be made only for the love of
work; not for money, not for art's sake, not
for intellectual appeal nor flippant ridicule, but for the pure love of things, good,
true and beautiful. With the best of in-
tentions we may fail; and this should be
laid down as a safe guiding principle; a
dramatist should be moved by his own
tragedy; the novelist should be interested
in his own story; the poet should make his
song for the love of the song and his
comedy for the fun of the thing.

VI

We naturally think of the Abbey Theatre when we speak of these things, and as the Abbey work has certainly suffered from overpraise we may correct it by comparison with Shakespeare. Before the Abbey we were so used to triviality that when clever and artistic work appeared we at once hailed it great. We *did* get one cr two great things, a fact to note with hearty pleasure and pride. But the rest was merely clever; and now that we are getting nothing great we must insist, and keep on insisting, that 'tis merely clever. But let us remember that value of the word great. Let it be kept for such names as Shakespeare and Molière; and lesser men may be called brilliant, talented or able—anything you will but great. Consider the scenes from the supreme plays of Shakespeare and compare with them the innumerable plays now coming forth and note a vital difference. These give us excitement, where Shakespeare gave us vision. We may be reminded of Shakespeare's duels and brawls and battles and blood; his generation revelled in excitement. Yes, they craved it, and he gave it

to them, but shot through with wonder,
subtlety, ecstasy; and his splendid crea-
tions, like mighty worlds, keep us wondering for ever. We must get back that
supreme note of blended music and
wonder, that makes the spirit beautiful
and tempts it to soar, till it rise over
common things and mere commotion,
spreading its wings for the finer air where
reason faints and falls to earth.

VII

A dramatist cannot make a great play
out of little people. His chief characters
at least must be great of heart and soul—
the great hearts that fight great causes.
When such are caught in the inevitable
struggle of affections and duties and the
general clash of life their passionate spirits
send up all the elements that make great
literature. The writer who cannot enter
into their battles and espouse their cause
cannot give utterance to their hearts; and
we don't want what he thinks about them;
we want what they think about themselves. He who is in passionate sympathy
with them feels their emotion and writing
from the heart does great things. The
artist who is in mortal dread of being

thought a politician or suspected of motives cannot feel, and will as surely
fail, as the one who sits down to play
the rôle of politician disguised as play-
right. That is what the artist has got to
see; and he has got to see that while
the Irish Revolution for centuries has
attracted the greatest hearts and brains of
Ireland, for him carefully to avoid it is to
avoid the line of greatness. For a propagandist to sit down to give it utterance
would be as if a handy-man were to set
out to build a cathedral. The Revolution
does not need to be argued; it justifies itself—all we need is to give it utterance—
give it utterance once greatly. Then the
writer may proceed to give utterance to
every good thing under the sun. But our
artists are making, and will continue to
make, only second-class literature, for they
are afraid of the Revolution, and it is all
over our best of life; they are afraid of that
life. But to enter the arena of greatness
they must give it a voice. That is the
vocation of the poet.

VIII

Yes, and the poet will be unlike you,
gentlemen of the fastidious phrase. He will

not be careless of form, but the passion that
is in him will make simple words burn and
live; never will he in the mode of the time
go wide of the truth to make a picturesque
phrase; his mind rapt on the thing will
fix on the true word; his heart warm with
the battle will fashion more beautiful
forms than you, O detached and dainty
artist; his soul full of music and adventure
will scale those heights it is your fate to
dream of but not your fortune to possess.
Yet, you, too, might possess them would
you but step with him into the press of
adventurous legions, and make articulate
the dream of men, and make splendid their
triumph. He is the prophet of to-morrow,
though you deny him to-day. He is not
like to you, supercilious and aloof—he
would have you for a passionate brother,
would raise your spirit in ecstasy, flood
your mind with thought, and touch your
lips with fire. Because of his sensitive-
ness he knows every mood and every heart
and gives a voice and a song to all. You
might know him for a good comrade, where
freedom is to win or to hold, over in the
va.i or the breach; able to deal good blows
and take them in the fine manner, a fine
fighter; not with darkened brow crying,

"an eye for an eye"—for who *could* give
him blow for blow or match his deed with a
deed?—but one of open front and open hand
who will count it happiness to have made
for a victory he may not live to enjoy, as
ready to die in its splendour as he had been
to live through the darkness before the
dawn; remembering with soldier tenderness the comrades of old battles, forgetting
the malice of old enemies; a high example
of the magnanimous spirit, happily not
yet unknown on earth; with fine gene-
rosity and noble fire, full of that great love
the common cry can never make other
than humanising and beautiful, not without a gleam of humour more than half
divine, he will pass, leaving to the foe that
hated him heartily equally with the friend
that loved him well, the wonder of his
thought and the rapture of his melody.

CHAPTER XII

RELIGION

I

IT ought to be laid down as a first principle that grave questions which have divided us in the past, and divide us still with much bitterness, should not be thrust aside and kept out of view in the hope of harmony. Where the attitude is such, the hope is vain. They should be approached with courage in the hope of creating mutual respect and an honourable solution for all. Religion is such a question. To the majority of men this touches their most intimate life. Because of their jealous regard for that intimate part of themselves they are prepared for bitter hostilities with anyone who will assail it; and because of the unmeasured bitterness

of assaults on all sides we have come to
count it a virtue to bring together in
societies labelled non-sectarian, men who
have been violently opposed on this issue.
It will be readily allowed that to bring
men together anyhow, even suspiciously,
is somewhat of an advance, when we keep
in mind how angrily they have quarrelled.
But 'tis not to our credit that in any
assembly a particular name hardly dare
be mentioned; and it must be realised that,
whatever purpose it may serve in lesser
undertakings, in the great fight for freedom
no such attitude will suffice. No grave
question can be settled by ignoring it.
Since it is our duty to make the War of
Independence a reality and a success, we
must invoke a contest that will as surely
rouse every latent passion and give every
latent suspicion an occasion and a field.
That is the danger ahead. We must anticipate that danger, meet and destroy it.
Perhaps at this suggestion most of us will
at once get restive. Some may say with
irritation : Why raise this matter? Others
on the other side may prepare forthwith
to dig up the hatchet. Is not the attitude
on both sides evidence of the danger?
Does anyone suppose we can start a fight

for freedom without making that danger
a grimmer reality? Who can claim it a
wise policy merely for the moment to
dodge it? For that is what we do. Let us
have courage and face it. At what I have
to say let no man take offence or fright—
it commits no one to anything. It is
written to try and make opponents understand and respect one another, not to set
them at one another, least of all to make
them "liberal," that is, lax and contemptible, ready to explain everything
away. We want primarily the man who is
prepared to fight his ground, but who is
big enough in heart and mind to respect
opponents who will also fight theirs. In
the integrity and courage of both sides is
the guarantee of the independence of both.
That should be our guiding thought. But as
on this question most people abandon all
tolerance, it is quite possible what may be
written will satisfy none; still, it may serve
the purpose of making a need apparent. To
repeat, we must face the question. But
whoever elects to start it, should approach
the issue with sympathy and forbearance.
These are as necessary as courage and resolution; yet, since many often sacrifice
firmness to sympathy, others will take the

opposite line of riding roughshod over
everyone, a harshness that confirms the
weakling in his weakness. To note all this
is but to note the difficulty; and if what is
now written fails in its appeal, it need only
be said to walk unerringly here would require the insight of a prophet and the
balance of an angel.

II

What everyone should take as a fair demand is that all men should be sincere in
their professions, and that we should
justify ourselves by the consistency of our
own lives rather than by the wickedness of
our neighbours : which is nothing new. It
is our trouble that we must emphasise
obvious duties. To approach the question
frankly with no matter what good faith
will lead to much heart-burning, perhaps,
to no little bitterness; but if we realise that
all sides are about equally to blame, we
may induce an earnestness that may lead
to better things. It is in that hope I write.
Catholics and Protestants, instead of saying to one another the things with which
we are familiar, should look to their own
houses; and if in this age of fashionable
agnosticism, they should conclude that the

M

enemy is the atheist, socialist, and
dicalist, they should still be re-
to look to their own houses; and
nostic take this to justify himself,
₁ₒ sɪould be reminded he has never done
anything to justify himself. It may seem
a curious way for inducing harmony to set
out to prove everyone in the wrong; but
the point is clear, not to attack what men
believe but to ask them to justify their
words by their deeds. The request is not
unreasonable and it may be asked in a tone
that will show the sincerity of him who
makes it and waken a kindred feeling in
all earnest men. The world will be a better
place to live in, and we shall be all better
friends when every man makes a genuine
resolve to give us all the example of a
better life.

III

A development that would require a
treatise in itself I will but touch on, to suggest to all interested a matter of general
and grave concern—the growing materialism of religious bodies. On all sides self-
constituted defenders of the faith are
troubling themselves, not with the faith
but with the numbers of their adherents

who have jobs, equal sharers in emoluments, and so forth. A Protestant of standing writes a book and proves his religion is one of efficiency; a Catholic of equal standing quickly rejoins with another book to prove his religion is also efficient; each blind to the fact that the resulting campaign is disgraceful to both. When religion ceases to represent to us something spiritual, and purely spiritual, we begin to drift away from it. "Where thy treasure is, there thy heart is also." "No man can serve God and Mammon." The modern rejoinder is familiar: "We must live." This, our generation is not likely to forget. The grave concern is that well-meaning men are accustoming themselves to this cry to sacrifice all higher considerations for the "equal division of emoluments." Let us as citizens and a community see that every man has the right and the means to live; but when self-interested bodies start a rivalry in the name of their particular creeds, we know it ends in a squalid greed and fight for place, in a pursuit of luxury, the logical outcome of which must be to make the world ugly, sordid and brutal. It would be a mistake to overlook that high-minded men are allowing themselves to be committed by plausible reasons to this growing evil. It is misguided enthusiasm. There is a divine authority that warns us all : "Be zealous for the better gifts."

IV

I wish to examine the attitude of the average Christian to the Agnostic. "The world is falling away from religion," he will cry when depressed, without thinking how much he himself may be a contributing cause. Let him study it in this light. What is his attitude? When he comes to speak of the tendency of the age he will indulge in vague generalities about atheism, socialism, irreligion, and the rest; always the cause is outside of him, and against him; he is not part of it. I ask him to pass by the atheist awhile and take what may be of more concern. There is a type of Catholic and Protestant who has as little genuine religion in him as any infidel, who does not deny the letter of the law, but who does not observe its spirit, whose only use for the letter is to criticise and harass adversaries. Observe the high use he has for liberty—drinking, card-playing, gambling, luxury; he has no place in his life for any worthy deeds, nay, only scorn for such. Still he passes for orthodox. If he is a Catholic, he secures that by putting in an appearance at Mass on Sundays. His mind is not there; he arrives late and goes early. His Protestant fellow in his private judgment finds more scope : "Let the women go listen to the parson." This is the sort of saying gives him such a conceit of himself. We have the type on both sides, so all can see it. Now it is not in the way of the Pharisee we come to note them, but to note that, strange as it may appear, either or both together will come to applaud the denouncing of the atheist. We gather such into our religious societies, and flatter them that they are adherents of religion and the bulwark of the faith, and they forthwith anathematise the atheist with great gusto. The one so anathematised is often as worthless as themselves with a conceit to despise priest and parson alike. But it sometimes happens he is a fine character who has no religion as most of us understand it, but who has yet a fine spiritual fervour, ready to fight and make sacrifices for a national or social principle that he believes will make for better things, a man of integrity and worth whom the best of men may be glad to hold as a friend. Yet we find in the condition to which we have drifted such a one may be pilloried by wasters, gamblers, rioters, a crew that are the curse of every community. We lash the atheist and the age but give little heed to the insincerity and cant of those we do not refuse to call our own. What an example for the man anathematised. He sees the vice and meanness of those we allow to pass for orthodox, and when he sees also the complacency of the better part, he is unconvinced. We praise the sweetness of the healing waters of Christ-like charity, but despite our gospel he never gets it, never. We give him execration, injustice; if we let him go with a word, it is never a gentle word, but a bitter epithet; and we wonder he is estranged, when he sees our amazing composure in an amazing welter of hypocrisy and deceit. There is, of course, the better side, the many thousands cf Catholics and Protestants who sincerely aim at better things. But what has to be admitted is that most sincerely religious people adopt to the man of no established religion the same attitude as does the hypocrite : they join in the general cry. They should look to their own houses; they should purge the temple of the money-lender and the knave; they should see that their field gives good harvest; they should remember that not to the atheist only but to the orthodox was it written : " Every tree therefore that doth not yield good fruit shall be cut down and cast into the fire."

V

There is a word to be said to the man for whom was invented the curious name agnostic. I'm concerned only with him who is sincere and high-minded. Let us pass the flippant critics of things they do not understand. But all sincere men are comrades in a deep and fine sense. What the honest unbeliever has to keep in mind is that the darker side is but one side. If he stands studying a crowd of the orthodox and finds therein the drunkard, the gambler, the sensualist; and if he says bitter things of the value of religion and gets in return the clerical fiat of one who is more a politician than a priest; and if he rejoins contemptuously, " This is fit for women and children," let him be reminded that he can also study the other side if he care. If he has the instinct of a fighter he must know every army has in its trail the camp-follower and the vulture, but when the battle is set and the danger is imminent, only the true soldier stands his ground. Because some who are of poor spirit are in high place, let him not forget the old spirit still exists. Not only the women but the best intellects of men still keep the old traditions. Newman and Pascal, Dante and Milton, Erigena and Aquinas, are all dead, but in our time even they have had followers not too far off. In the same spirit Gilbert Chesterton found wonder at a wooden post, and Francis Thompson, in his divine wandering, troubled the gold gateways of the stars. Let our friend before he frames his final judgment pause here. He may well be baffled by many anomalies of the time, his eye may rest on the meaner horde, his ear be filled with the arrogance of some unworthy successor of Paul; and if he says : "Why permit these things?" he may be told there are some alive in this generation who will question all such things, and who, however hard it go with them, have no fear for the final victory.

VI

Perhaps the conventional Christian and conventional non-Christian may rest a moment to consider the reality. Between the bitter believer and the exasperated unbeliever, Christianity is being turned from a practice to a polemic, and if we are to recall the old spirit we must recall the old earnestness and simplicity of the early Martyrs. We do not hear that they called Nero an atheist, but we do hear that they went singing to the arena. By their example we may recover the spirit of song, and have done with invective. If we find music and joyousness in the old conception, it is not in the fashion of the time to explain it away in some "new theology," for he to whom it is not a fashion, but a vital thing, keeps his anchor by tradition. To him it is the shining light away in the mists of antiquity; it is the strong sun over the living world; it is the pillar of fire over the widening seas and worlds of the unknown; it is the expanse of infinity. When he is lost in its mystery he adverts to the wonder about him, for all that is wonderful is touched with it, and all that is lovely is its expression. It is in the breath of the wind, pure and bracing from the mountain top. It is in the song of the lark holding his musical revel in the sunlight. It is in the ecstasy of a Spring morning. It is in the glory of all beautiful things. When it has entered and purified his spirit, his heart goes out to the persecuted in all ages and countries. None will he reject. "I am not come to call the just but sinners." He remembers those words, and his great charity encompasses not only the persecuted orthodox, but the persecuted heretics and infidels.

VII

I will not say if such an endeavour as I suggest can have an immediate success. But I think it will be a step forward if we get sincere men on one side to understand the sincerity of the other side; and if in matters of religion and speculation, where there is so much difficulty and there is likely to be so much conflict of opinion, there should be no constraint, but rather the finest charity and forbearance; then the orthodox would be concerned with practising their faith rather than in harassing the infidel, and the infidel would receive a more useful lesson than the ill-considered tirades he despises. He may remain still unconvinced, but he will give over his contempt. This question of religion is one on which men will differ, and differing, ultimately they will fight if we find no better way. We must remember while freedom is to win we are facing a national struggle, and if we are threatened within by a civil war of creeds it may undo us. That is why we must face the question. That is why I think utter frankness in these grave matters is of grave urgency. If we approach them in the right spirit we need have no fear—for at heart the most of men are susceptible to high appeals. What we need is courage and intensity; it is gabbling about surface things makes the bitterness. If in truth we safeguard the right of every man as we are bound to do we shall win the confidence of all, and we may hope for a braver and better future, wherein some light of the primal Beauty may wander again over earth as in the beginning it dawned on chaos when the Spirit of God first moved over the waters.

CHAPTER XIII

INTELLECTUAL FREEDOM

I

IT will probably cause surprise if I say
there is, possibly, more intellectual freedom in Ireland than elsewhere in Europe.
But I do not mean by intellectual freedom conventional Free-thought, which is,
perhaps, as far as any superstition from
true freedom of the mind. The point may
not be admitted but its consideration will
clear the air, and help to dispose of some
objections hindering that spiritual freedom, fundamental to all liberty.

II

I have no intention here of in any way
criticising the doctrine of Free-thought,
but one so named cannot be ignored when

we consider Intellectual Freedom. This, then, has to be borne in mind when speaking of Free-thought, that while it allows you latitude of opinion in many things, it will not allow you freedom in all things, in, for example, Revealed Religion. I only mention this to show that on both sides of such burning questions you have disputants dogmatic. A dogmatic "yes" meets an equally dogmatic "no." The dogmas differ and it is not part of our business here to discuss them : but to come to a clear conception of the matter in hand, it must be kept in mind, that if you, notwithstanding, freely of your own accord, accept belief in certain doctrines, the freethinkers will for that deny you freedom. And the freethinkers are right in that they are dogmatic. (But this they themselves appear to overlook.) Freedom is absolutely dogmatic. It is fundamentally false that freedom implies no attachment to any belief, no being bound by any law, "As free as the wind," as the saying goes, for the wind is not free. Simple indeterminism is not liberty.

III

We must, then, find the true conception
of Intellectual Freedom. It is the freedom
of the individual to follow his star and
reach his goal. That star binds him down to
certain lines and his freedom is in exact
proportion to his fidelity to the lines. The
seeming paradox may be puzzling : a concrete example will make it clear. Suppose
a man, shipwrecked, finds himself at sea
in an open boat, without his bearings or a
rudder. He is at the mercy of the wind
and wave, without freedom, helpless. But
give him his bearings and a helm, and at
once he recovers his course; he finds his
position and can strike the path to freedom. He is at perfect liberty to scuttle his
boat, drive it on the rocks or do any other
irrational thing; but if he would have freedom, he must follow his star.

IV

This leads us to track a certain error that
has confused modern debate. A man in
assumed impartiality tells you he will
stand away from his own viewpoint and
consider a case from yours. Now, if he

does honestly hold by his own view and thinks he can put it by and judge from his opponent's, he is deceiving both himself and his opponent. He can do so *apparently*, but, whatever assumption is made, he is governed subconsciously by his own firm conviction. His belief is around him like an atmosphere; it goes with him wherever he goes; he can only stand free of it by altogether abandoning it. If his case is such that he can come absolutely to the other side to view it uninfluenced by his own, then he has abandoned his own. He is like a man in a boat who has thrown over rudder and bearings : he may be moved by any current : he is adrift. If he is to recover the old ground, he must win it as something he never had. But if instead of this he does at heart hold by his own view, he should give over the deception that he is uninfluenced by it in framing judgment. It is psychologically impossible. Let the man understand it as a duty to himself to be just to others, and to substitute this principle for his spurious impartiality. This is the frank and straightforward course. While he is under his own star, he is moving in its light : he has, if unconsciously, his hand on the helm : he judges all currents scrupulously and exactly, but always from his own place at the wheel and with his own eyes. To abandon one or the other is to betray his trust, or in good faith and ignorance to cast it off till it is gone, perhaps, too far to recover.

v

If we so understand intellectual freedom, in what does its denial consist? In this : around every set of principles guiding men, there grows up a corresponding set of prejudices that with the majority in practice often supersede the principles; and these prejudices with the march of time assume such proportions, gather such power, both by the numbers of their adherents and the authority of many supporting them, that for a man of spirit, knowing them to be evil and urgent of resistance, there is needed a vigour and freedom of mind that but few understand and even fewer appreciate or encourage. The prejudices that grow around a man's principles are like weeds and poison in his garden : they blight his flowers, trees and fruit; and he must go forth with fire and sword and strong unsparing hand to root

out the evil things. He will find with his
courage and strength are needed passion
and patience and dogged persistence. For
men defend a prejudice with bitter venom
altogether unlike the fire that quickens the
fighter for freedom; and the destroyer of
the evil may find himself assailed by an
astonishing combination—charged with
bad faith or treachery or vanity or sheer
perversity, in proportion as those who dis-
like his principles deny his good faith; or
those who profess them, because of his
vigour and candour denounce him for an
enemy within the fold. But for all that he
should stand fast. If he has the courage
so to do, he gives a fine example of intellectual freedom.

VI

It will serve us to consider some prejudices, free-thinking and religious. First
the free-thinker. He has a prejudice very
hard to kill. If I believe in the beginning
what Bernard Shaw has found out thus
late in the day, that priests are not as bad
as they are painted, the free-thinker would
deny me intellectual freedom. The fact of
my right to think the matter out and come
to that conclusion would count for noth-

N

ing. On the other hand, if I were known to have professed a certain faith and to have abandoned it, he would acclaim that as casting off mental slavery. This is hopelessly confusing. If a man has ceased to hold a certain belief he deserves no credit for courage in saying so openly. If he thinks what he once believed, or is supposed to have believed, has no vitality, surely he can have no reason for being afraid of it, and to speak of dangerous consequences from it to him, can be *for him* at least only a bogey. His simple denial is, then, no mark of courage. Courage is a positive thing. Yet he may well have that courage. Suppose him in taking his stand to have taken up some social faith that for him has promise of better things. He will find his new creed surrounded by its own swarm of prejudices, and if he refuse to worship every fetish of the free-thinker, declaring that this stands to him for a certain definite, beautiful thing, and fighting for it, he will find himself denied and scouted by his new friends. He may find himself often in company with some supposed enemies. He will surely need in his sincere attitude to life a freedom of mind that is not a name merely but a positive virtue that demands of him more than denunciation of obscurantism, the recognition of a personal duty and the justification of personal works.

The religious prejudice will be no less hard to kill. Indiscriminate denunciation of unbelievers as wicked men serves no good purpose and leads nowhere. There are wicked men on all sides. Our standard must be one that will distinguish the sincere men on all sides; and our loyalty to our particular creeds must be shown in our lives and labours, not in the reviling of the infidel. We are justified in casting out the hypocrite from every camp, and when we come to this task we can be sure only of the hypocrites in our own; and we should lay it as an injunction on all bodies to purge themselves. The burden will be laid on all—not one surely of which men can complain—that they shall prove their principles in action and lay their prejudices by. Christians might well find exemplars in the early martyrs, those who for their principles went so readily to the lions. One may anticipate the complacent

rejoinder : " This is not so exacting an age;
men are not asked to die for religion now "
—and one may in turn reply, that, perhaps
our age may not be without occasion for
such high service, but that we may be unwilling to go to the lions. Our time has
its own trial—by no means unexacting let
me tell you—but we quietly slip it by : it is
much easier to revile the infidel. This as
a test of loyalty should be pinned : we shall
shut up thereby the hypocrite. And the
earnest man, more conscious of his own
burden, will be more sympathetic, generous
and just, and will come to be more logical
and to see what Newman well remarked,
that one who asks questions shows he has
no belief and in asking may be but on the
road to one. If to ask a question is to
express a doubt, it is no less, perhaps, to
seek a way out of it. " What better can
he do than inquire, if he is in doubt?" asks
Newman. " Not to inquire is in his case to
be satisfied with disbelief." We should,
acting in this light, instead of denouncing
the questioner, answer his question freely
and frankly, encourage him to ask others
and put him one or two by the way. Men
meeting in this manner may still remain
on opposite sides, but there will be formed

between them a bond of sympathy that mutual sincerity can never fail to establish. This is freedom, and a fine beautiful thing, surely worth a fine effort. What we have grown accustomed to, the bitterness, the recriminations, the persecutions and retaliations, are all the evil weeds of prejudice, growing around our principles and choking them. They are so far a denial of principle, a proof of mental slavery. Our freedom will attest to faith : "Where the Spirit of the Lord is, there is Liberty."

VIII

This, in conclusion, is the root of the matter : to claim freedom and to allow it in like measure; rather than to deny, to urge men to follow their beliefs : only thus can they find salvation. To constrain a man to profess what we profess is worse than delusion : should he give lip service to what he does not hold at heart, 'twere for him deceitful and for us dangerous. Where his star calls, let him walk sincerely. If his creed is insufficient or inconsistent, in his struggle he shall test it, and in his sincerity he must make up the insufficiency or remove the inconsistency.

This is the only course for honourable men and no man should object. To repeat, it puts an equal burden on all—the onus of justifying the faith that is in them. Life is a divine adventure and he whose faith is finest, firmest and clearest will go farthest. God does not hold his honours for the timid : the man who buried his talent, fearing to lose it, was cast into exterior darkness. He who will step forward fearlessly will be justified. "All things are possible to him who believeth." Many on both sides may be surprised to find suddenly proposed as a test to both sides the readiness to adventure bravely on the Sea of Life. The free-thinker may be astonished to hear, not that he goes too far, but does not go far enough. He may gasp at the test, but it is in effect the test and the only true one. The man who does not believe he is to be blotted out when his body ceases to breathe, who holds all history for his heritage and the wide present for his battle-ground, believes also the future is no repellent void but a widening and alluring world. If in his travel he is scrupulous in detail, it is in the spirit of the mariner who will neither court a shipwreck nor be denied his adventure. He cannot deny to others the right to hesitate and halt by the way, but his spirit asks no less than the eternal and the infinite. Yes, but many good religious people are not used to seeing the issue in this light, and those who make a trade of fanning old bitterness will still ply their bitter trade, crying that anarchists, atheists, heretics, infidels, all outcasts and wicked men, are all rampant for our destruction. It may be disputed, but, admitting it, one may ask : Is there no place among Christian people for those distinctive virtues on which we base the superiority of our religion? When the need is greatest, should the practice be less urgent? It is not evident that the freethinker is obliged by any of his principles to give better example. It is evident the Christian is so obliged. Why is he found wanting? If human weakness were pleaded, one could understand. It is against the making a virtue of it lies the protest. How many noble things there are in our philosophies, and how little practised. No violent convulsions should be needed to make us free, if men were but consistent : we should find ourselves wakening from a wicked dream in a bloodless and beautiful revolution. We are in the desert truly and a long way from the Promised Land. But we must get to the higher ground and consider our position; and if one by one we are stripped of the prejudices that too long have usurped the place of faith, and we find ourselves, to our dismay, perhaps lacking that faith that we have so long shouted but so little testified, and tremble on the verge of panic, there is one last line that gives in four words with divine simplicity and completeness a final answer to all timidity and objections : "Fear not; only believe."

CHAPTER XIV

MILITARISM

I

TO defend or recover freedom men must be always ready for the appeal to arms. Here is a principle that has been vindicated through all history and needs vindication now. But in our time the question of rightful war has been crossed by the evil of militarism, and in our assertion of the principle, that in the last resort freemen must have recourse to the sword, we find ourselves crossed by the anti-militarist campaign. We must dispose of this confusing element before we can come to the ethics of war. Of the evil of militarism there can be no question, but a careful study of some anti-militaristic literature discloses very different motives for the campaign. I propose to lay some of the motives bare and let the reader judge whether there may not be an insidious plot on foot to make a deal between the big nations to crush the little ones. For this purpose I will consider two books on the question, one by Mr. Norman Angell, "The Great Illusion," and one by M. Jacques Novikow, "War and Its Alleged Benefits." In the work of Mr. Angell the reader will find the suggestion of the deal, while in the work of M. Novikow is given a clear and honest statement of the anti-militarist position, with which we can all heartily agree. Those of us who would assert our freedom should understand the right anti-militarist position, because in its exponents we shall find allies at many points. But with Mr. Angell's book it is otherwise. These points emerge : the basis of morality is self-interest; the Great Powers have nothing to gain by destroying one another, they should agree to police and exploit the territory of the "backward races"; if the statesmen take a different view from the financiers, the financiers can bring pressure to bear on the statesmen by their international organisation; the capitalist has no country. Well, our comment is, the patriot has a country, and when he wakens to the new danger, he may spoil the capitalist dream, and this book of Mr. Angell's may in a sense other than that the author intended be appropriately named ' The Great Illusion."

II

The limits of this essay do not admit of detailed examination of the book named. What I propose to do is make characteristic extracts sufficiently full to let the reader form judgment. As we are only concerned for the present with the danger I mention, I take particular notice of Mr. Angell's book, and I refer the reader for further study to the original. But the charge of taking an accidental line from its context cannot be made here, as the extracts are numerous, the tendency of all alike, and more of the same nature can be found. I divide the extracts into three groups, which I name :

1. The Ethics of the Case.
2. The Power of Money.
3. The Deal.

Where italics are used they are mine.

1. THE ETHICS OF THE CASE.—" The real basis of Social Morality is self-

interest." ("The Great Illusion," 3rd Ed., p. 66.) "Have we not abundant evidence, indeed, that the passion of patriotism, as divorced from material interest, is being modified by the pressure of material interest?" (p. 167.) "Piracy was magnificent, doubtless, but it was not business." (Speaking of the old Vikings, p. 245.) "The pacifist propaganda has failed largely because it has not put (and proven) the plea of interest as distinct from the moral plea." (p. 321.)

2. THE POWER OF MONEY —"The complexity of modern finance makes New York dependent on London, London upon Paris, Paris upon Berlin, to a greater degree than has ever yet been the case in history." (p. 47.)

"It would be a miracle if already at this point the whole influence of British Finance were not thrown against the action of the British Government." (On the assumed British capture of Hamburg, p. 53).

"The most absolute despots cannot command money." (p. 226.)

"With reference to capital, it may almost be said that it is organised so naturally internationally that *formal organisation is not necessary*." (p. 269.)

3. THE DEAL.—" France has benefited by the conquest of Algeria, England by that of India, because in each case the arms were employed not, properly speaking, for conquest at all, but *for police purposes.*" (p. 115.)

"While even the wildest Pan-German has never cast his eyes in the direction of Canada, he has cast them, and does cast them, in the direction of Asia Minor. . . . . *Germany may need to police Asia Minor.*" (pp. 117, 118.)

"*It is much more to our interest to have an orderly and organised Asia Minor under German tutelage than to have an unorganised and disorderly one which should be independent.*" (p. 120.)

" Sir Harry Johnston, in the 'Nineteenth Century' for December, 1910, comes a great deal nearer to touching the real kernel of the problem. . . . He adds that the best informed Germans used this language to him : ' *You know that we ought to make common cause in our dealings with backward races of the world !*' "

The quotations speak for themselves. Note the policing of the " backward races." The Colonies are not in favour. Mr. Angell writes : " What in the name of

common sense is the advantage of conquering them if the only policy is to let
them do as they like?" (p. 92.) South
Africa occasions bitter reflections : "The
present Government of the Transvaal is in
the hands of the Boer Party." (p. 95.) And
he warns Germany, that, supposing she
wishes to conquer South Africa, "she would
learn that the policy that Great Britain has
adopted was not adopted by philanthropy,
but in the hard school of bitter experience."
(p. 104.) We believe him, and we may
have to teach a lesson or two in the same
school. It may be noted in passing Mr.
Angell gives Ireland the honcur of a
reference. In reply to a critic of the
Morning Post, who wrote thus : "It is the
sublime quality of human nature that
every great nation has produced citizens
ready to sacrifice themselves rather than
submit to external force attempting to dictate to them a conception other than their
own of what is right." (p. 254.) Mr. Angell
replied : "One is, of course, surprised to see
the foregoing in the *Morning Post*; the
concluding phrase would justify the
present agitation in India, or in Egypt, or
in Ireland against British rule." (p. 254.)
Comment is needless. The reading and re-

reading of this book forces the conclusion as to its sinister design. Once that design is exposed its danger recedes. There is one at least of the "backward races" that may not be sufficiently alive to self-interest, but may for all that upset the capitalist table and scatter the deal by what Ruskin described in another context as "the inconvenience of the reappearance of a soul."

III

We must not fail to distinguish the worth of the best type of anti-militarist and to value the truth of his statement. It is curious to find Mr. Angell writing an introduction to M. Novikow's book, for M. Novikow's position is, in our point of view, quite different. He does not draw the fine distinction of policing the "backward races." Rather, he defends the Bengalis. Suppose their rights had never been violated, he says : "They would have held their heads higher; they would have been proud and dignified, and perhaps might have taken for their motto, *Dieu et mon droit*." ("War and Its Alleged Benefits," p. 12.) He can be ironical and he can be warm. Later, he writes : "The French (and

all other people) should vindicate their
rights with their last drop of blood; so
what I write does not refer to those who
defend their rights, but to those who
violate the rights of others." (Note p. 70.)
He does not put by the moral plea, but
says : "Political servitude develops the
greatest defects in the subjugated peoples."
(p. 79.) And he pays his tribute to those
who die for a noble cause : "My warmest
sympathy goes out to those noble victims
who preferred death to disgrace." (p. 82.)
This is the true attitude and one to admire;
and any writer worthy of esteem who
writes for peace never fails to take the
same stand.   Emerson, in his essay on
" War," makes a fine appeal for peace, but
he writes : "If peace is sought to be de-
fended or preserved for the safety of the
luxurious or the timid, it is a sham and
the peace will be base. War is better, and
the peace will be broken." And elsewhere
on " Politics," he writes : "A nation of men
unanimously bent on freedom or conquest
can easily confound the arithmetic of the
statists and achieve extravagant actions
out of all proportions to their means." Yes,
and by our unanimity for freedom we
mean to prove it true.

CHAPTER XV

THE EMPIRE

I

WITH the immediate promise of Home Rule many strange apologists for the Empire have stepped into the sun. Perhaps it is well—we may find ourselves soon more directly than heretofore struggling with the Empire. So far the fight has been confused. Imperialists fighting for Home Rule obscured the fact that they were *not* fighting the Empire. Now Home Rule is likely to come, and it will serve at least the good purpose of clearing the air and setting the issue definitely between the nation and the Empire. We shall have our say for the nation, but as even now many things, false and hypocritical, are being urged on behalf of the Empire, it will serve us to examine the Imperial creed and show its tyranny, cruelty, hypocrisy, and expose the danger of giving it any pretext whatever for aggression. For the Empire, as we know it and deal with it, is a bad thing in itself, and we must not only get free of it and not be again trapped by it, but must rather give hope and encouragement to every nation fighting the same fight all the world over.

II

One candid writer, Machiavelli, has put the Imperial creed into a book, the examination of which will—for those willing to see—clear the air of illusion. Now, we are conscious that defenders of the Empire profess to be shocked by the wickedness of Machiavelli's utterance—we shall hear Macaulay later—but this shocked attitude won't delude us. Let those who have not read Machiavelli's book, "The Prince," consider carefully the extracts given below and see exactly how they fit the English occupation of Ireland, and understand thoroughly that the Empire is a thing, bad in itself, utterly wicked, to be resisted everywhere, fought without ceasing, renounced with fervour and without qualification, as we have been taught from the cradle to renounce the Devil with all his works and pomps. Consider first the invasion. Machiavelli speaks :—"The common method in such cases is this. As soon as a foreign potentate enters into a province those who are weaker or dis-obliged join themselves with him out of emulation and animosity to those who are above them, insomuch that in respect to those inferior lords no pains are to be omitted that may gain them; and when gained, they will readily and unanimously fall into one mass with the State that is conquered. Only the conqueror is to take special care that they grow not too strong, nor be entrusted with too much authority, and then he can easily with his own forces and their assistance keep down the great-ness of his neighbours, and make himself absolute arbiter in that province." Here is the old maxim, "Divide and conquer." To gain an entry some pretence is advis-able. Machiavelli speaks with approval of a certain potentate who always made religion a pretence. Having entered a vigorous policy must be pursued. We read—" He who usurps the government of

any State is to execute and put in practice
all the cruelties which he thinks material
at once." Cromwell rises before us.

"A prince," says Machiavelli, "is not to
regard the scandal of being cruel if thereby
he keeps his subjects in their allegiance."
"For," he is cautioned, "whoever conquers
a free town and does not demolish it commits a great error and may expect to be
ruined himself; because whenever the citizens are disposed to revolt they betake
themselves, of course, to that blessed name
of Liberty, and the laws of their ancestors,
which no length of time nor kind usage
whatever will be able to eradicate." An
alternative to utter destruction is flattery
and indulgence. "Men are either to be
flattered and indulged or utterly de-
stroyed." We think of the titles and the
bribes. Again, "A town that has been
anciently free cannot more easily be kept
in subjection than by employing its own
citizens." We think of the place-hunter,
the King's visit, the "loyal" address. To
make the conquest secure we read : "When
a prince conquers a new State and annexes
it as a member to his old, then it is necessary your subjects be disarmed, all but
such as appeared for you in the conquest,

and they are to be mollified by degrees and brought into such a condition of laziness and effeminacy that in time your whole strength may devolve ⁃upon your own natural militia." We think of the Arms Acts and our weakened people. But while one-half is disarmed and the other half bribed, with neither need the conqueror keep faith. We read : " A prince who is wise and prudent cannot, or ought not, to keep his parole, when the keeping of it is to his prejudice and the causes for which he promised removed." This is made very clear to prevent any mistake. "It is of great consequence to disguise your inclination and play the hypocrite well." We think of the Broken Treaty and countless other breaches of faith. It is, of course, well to seem honourable, but Machiavelli cautions : "It is honourable to seem mild, and merciful, and courteous, and religious, and sincere, and indeed to be so, provided your mind be so rectified and prepared, that you can act quite contrary upon occasion." Should anyone hesitate at all this let him hear : " He is not to concern himself if run under the infamy of those vices, without which his dominion was not to be preserved." Thus far the philosophy

of Machiavelli. The Imperialist out to
"civilise the barbarians" is, of course,
shocked by such wickedness; but we are
beginning to open our eyes to the wickedness and hypocrisy of both. To us this
book reads as if a shrewd observer of the
English Occupation in Ireland had noted
the attending features and based these
principles thereon. We have reason to be
grateful to Machiavelli for his exposition.
His advice to the prince, in effect, lays bare
the marauders of his age and helps us to
expose the Empire in our own.

III

There is a lesson to be learnt from the
fact that this book of Machiavelli's, written
four centuries ago in Italy, is so apt here
to-day. We must take this exposition as
the creed of Empire and have no truck
with the Empire. It may be argued that
the old arts will be no longer practised on
us. Let the new supporters of the Empire
know that by the new alliance they should
practise these arts on other people, which
would be infamy. We are not going to
hold other people down; we are going to
encourage them to stand up. If it means a
further fight we have plenty of stimulus

still. Our oppression has been doubly bitter for having been mean. The tyranny of a strong mind makes us rage, but the tyranny of a mean one is altogether insufferable. The cruelty of a Cromwell can be forgotten more easily than the cant of a Macaulay. When we read certain lines we go into a blaze, and that fire will burn till it has burnt every opposition out. In his essay on Milton, Macaulay having written much bombast on the English Revolution, introduces this characteristic sentiment : " One part of the Empire there was, so unhappily circumstanced, that at that time its misery was necessary to our happiness and its slavery to our freedom." For insolence this would be hard to beat. Let it be noted well. It is the philosophy of the " Predominant Partner." If he had thanked God for having our throats to cut, and cut them with loud gratitude like Cromwell, a later generation would be incensed. But this other attitude is the gall in the cup. Macaulay is, of course, shocked by Machiavelli's " Prince." In his essay on Machiavelli we read : " It is indeed scarcely possible for any person not well acquainted with the history and literature of Italy to read without horror and amaze-

ment the celebrated treatise which has
brought so much obloquy on the name of
Machiavelli. Such a display of wickedness, naked, yet not ashamed, such cool,
judicious, scientific atrocity, seemed rather
to belong to a fiend than to the most de-
praved of men." But, later, in the same
essay, is a valuable sidelight. He writes of
Machiavelli as a man "whose only fault
was that, having adopted some of the
maxims then generally received, he
arranged them most luminously and ex-
pressed them more forcibly than any other
writer." Here we have the truth, of course
not so intended, but evident : Machiavelli's
crime is not for the sentiments he entertained but for writing them down
luminously and forcibly—in other words,
for giving the show away.

Think of Macaulay's "horror and
amazement," and read this further in the
same essay : "Every man who has seen the
world knows that nothing is so useless as a
general maxim. If it be very moral and
very true it may serve for a copy to a
charity boy." So the very moral and the
very true are not for the statesman but for
the charity-boy. This perhaps may be de-
fended as irony; hardly, but even so, in

such irony the character appears as plainly
as in volumes of solemn rant. To us it
stands out clearly as the characteristic
attitude of the English Government. The
English people are used to it, practise it,
and will put up with it; but the Irish
people never were, are not now, and never
will be used to it; and we won't put up
with it. We get calm as old atrocities
recede into history, but to repeat the old
cant, above all to try and sustain such now,
sets all the old fire blazing—blazing with a
fierceness that will end only with the
British connection.

IV

Not many of us in Ireland will be de-
ceived by Macaulay, but there is danger in
an occasional note of writers, such as Bernard Shaw and Stuart Mill. Our instinct
often saves us by natural repugnance from
the hypocrite, when we may be confused
by some sentiment of a sincere man, not
foreseeing its tendency. When an aggressive power looks for an opening for aggression it first looks for a pretext, and our
danger lies in men's readiness to give it the
pretext. Such a sentiment as this from
Mill—on "Liberty"—gives the required

opening : "Despotism is a legitimate mode
of government in dealing with Barbarians,
provided the end be their improvement";
or this from Shaw's preface to the Home
Rule edition of "John Bull's Other
Island": "I am prepared to Steam-roll
Tibet if Tibet persist in refusing me my
international rights." Now, it is within our
right to enforce a principle within our own
territory, but to force it on other people,
called for the occasion "barbarians," is
quite another thing. Shaw may get wrath-
ful, and genuinely so, over the Denshawai
horror, and expose it nakedly and vividly
as he did in his first edition of "John Bull's
Other Island," Preface for Politicians; but
the aggressors are undisturbed as long as
he gives them pretexts with his "steam-
roll Tibet" phrase. And when he says further that he is prepared to co-operate with
France, Italy, Russia, Germany and England in Morocco, Tripoli, Siberia and
Africa to civilise these places, not only are
his denunciations of Denshawai horrors of
no avail—except to draw tears after the
event—but he cannot co-operate in the
civilising process without practising the
cruelty; and perhaps in their privacy the
empire-makers may smile when Shaw

writes of Empire with evident earnestness as " a name that every man who has ever felt the sacredness of his own native soil to him, and thus learnt to regard that feeling in other men as something holy and inviolable, spits out of his mouth with enormous contempt." When, further, in his "Representative Government" Mill tells the English people—a thing about which Shaw has no illusions—that they are "the power which of all in existence best understands liberty, and, whatever may have been its errors in the past, has attained to more of conscience and moral principle in its dealing with foreigners than any other great nation seems either to conceive as possible or recognise as desirable"—they not only go forward to civilise the barbarians by Denshawai horrors, but they do so unctuously in the true Macaulayan style. We feel a natural wrath at all this, not unmingled with amusement and amazement. In studying the question we read much that rouses anger and contempt, but one must laugh out heartily in coming to this gem of Mill's, uttered with all Mill's solemnity : "Place-hunting is a form of ambition to which the English, considered nationally, are almost

strangers." When the sincerest expression
of the English mind can produce this we
need to have our wits about us; and
when, as just now, so much nonsense, and
dangerous nonsense, is being poured
abroad about the Empire, we need to
pause, carefully consider all these things,
and be on our guard.

V

In conclusion, we may add our own word
to the talk of the hour—the politicians on
Home Rule. It should raise a smile to hear
so often the prophecy that Ireland will be
loyal to the Empire when she gets Home
Rule. We are surprised that any Irishman
could be so foolish, though, no doubt, many
Englishmen are so simple as to believe it.
History and experience alike deny it. Possibly the Home Rule chiefs realise their
active service is now limited to a decade or
two, and assume Home Rule may be the
limit for that time, and speak only for that
time; but at the end of that time our
generation will be vigorous and com-
bative, and if we cannot come into our own
before then, we shall be ready then. We
need say for the moment no more than this

—the limit of the old generation is not the limit of ours. If anyone doubt the further step to take let him consider our history, recent and remote. The old effort to subdue or exterminate us having failed, the new effort to conciliate us began. Minor concessions led to the bigger question of the land. One Land Act led to another till the people came by their own. Home Rule, first to be killed by resolute government, was next to be killed by kindness, and Local Government came. Local Government made Home Rule inevitable; and now Home Rule is at hand and we come to the last step. Anyone who reads the history of Ireland, who understands anything of progress, who can draw any lesson from experience, must realise that the advent of Home Rule marks the beginning of the end.

CHAPTER XVI

RESISTANCE IN ARMS—FOREWORD

I

THE discussion of freedom leads in-evitably to the discussion of an appeal to arms. If proving the truth and justice of a people's claim were sufficient there would be little tyranny in the world, but a tyrannical power is deaf to the appeal of truth—it cannot be moved by argument, and must be met by force. The discussion of the ethics of revolt is, then, inevitable.

II

The ubiquitous pseudo-practical man, petulant and critical, will at once arise: "What is the use of discussing arms in Ireland? If anyone wanted to fight it

would be impossible, and no one wants to
fight. What prevents ye going out to begin?" Such peevish criticism is anything
but practical, and one may ignore it; but
it suggests the many who would earnestly
wish to settle our long war with a swift,
conclusive fight, yet who feel it no longer
practical. Keeping to the practical issue,
we must bear in mind a few things.
Though Ireland has often fought at odds,
and could do so again, it is not just now a
question of Ireland poorly equipped standing up to England invincible. England
will never again have such an easy battle.
The point now to emphasise is this—by
remaining passive and letting ourselves
drift we drift into the conflict that involves
England. We must fight for her or get
clear of her. There can be no neutrality
while bound to her; so a military policy is
an eminently practical question. More-
over, it is an urgent one : to stand in with
England in any danger that threatens her
will be at least as dangerous as a bold bid
to break away from her. One thing above
all, conditions have changed in a startling
manner; England is threatened within as
without; there are labour complications of
all kinds of which no one can foresee the

end, while as a result of another complication we find the Prime Minister of England going about as carefully protected as the Czar of Russia.* The unrest of the times is apt to be even bewildering. England is not alone in her troubles—all the great Powers are likewise; and it is at least as likely for any one of them to be paralysed by an internal war as to be prepared to wage an external one. This stands put clearly—we cannot go away from the turmoil and sit down undisturbed; we must stand in and fight for our own hand or the hand of someone else. Let us prepare and stand for our own. However it be, no one can deny that in all the present upheavals it is at least practical to discuss the ethics of revolt.

III

We can count on a minority who will see wisdom in such a discussion; it must be our aim to make the discussion effective. We must be patient as well as resolute. We are apt to get impatient and by hasty denunciation drive off many who are wavering and may be won. These are held back, perhaps, by some scruple or nervous-

* The militant suffragette agitation.

ness, and by a fine breath of the truth and a natural discipline may yet be made our truest soldiers. Emerson, in his address at the dedication of the Soldiers' Monument, Concord, made touching reference to some such in the American Civil War. He told of one youth he knew who feared he was a coward, and yet accustomed himself to danger, by forcing himself to go and meet it. "He enlisted in New York," says Emerson, "went out to the field, and died early." And his comment for us should be eloquent. "It is from this temperament of sensibility that great heroes have been formed." The pains we are at to make men physically fit we must take likewise to make them mentally fit. We are minutely careful in physical training, drill regulations and the rest, which is right, for thus we turn a mob into an army and helplessness into strength. Let us be minutely careful, too, with the untried minds— timid, anxious, sensitive in matters of conscience; like him Emerson spoke of, they may be found yet in the foremost fighting line, but we must have patience in pleading with them. Here above all must we keep our balance, must we come down with sympathy to every particular. It is surely

P

evident that it is essential to give the care we lavish on the body with equal fulness to the mind.

IV

At the heart of the question we will be met by the religious objection to revolt. Here all scruples, timidity, wavering, will concentrate; and here is our chief difficulty to face. The right to war is invariably allowed to independent states. The right to rebel, even with just cause, is not by any means invariably allowed to subject nations. It has been and is denied to us in Ireland. We must answer objectors line by line, leading them, where it serves, step by step to our conclusions; but this is not to make freedom a mere matter of logic —it is something more. When it comes to war we shall frequently give, not our promises, but our conclusions. This much must be allowed, however, that, as far as logic will carry, our position must be perfectly sound; yet, be it borne in mind, our cause reaches above mere reasoning—mere logic does not enshrine the mysterious touch of fire that is our life. So, when we argue with opponents we undertake to give them as good as or better than they can

give, but we stake our cause on the something that is more. On this ground I argue
not in general on the right of war, but in
particular on the right of revolt; not how
it may touch other people elsewhere ignoring how it touches us here in Ireland. A
large treatise could be written on the
general question, but to avoid seeming
academic I will confine myself as far as
possible to the side that is our concern.
For obvious reasons I propose to speak as
to how it affects Catholics, and let them
and others know what some Catholic
writers of authority have said on the
matter. One thing has to be carefully
made clear. It is seen in the following
quotation from an eminent Catholic authority writing in Ireland in the middle of the
last century, Dr. Murray, of Maynooth :
"The Church has issued no definition
whatever on the question—has left it open.
Many theologians have written on it; the
great majority, however (so far as I have
been able to examine them), pass it over
in silence." (*Essays chiefly Theological*,
vol. 4). This has to be kept in mind. Theologians have written, some on one side and
some on the other, but the Church has left
it open. I need not labour the point why

it is useful to quote Catholic authorities in particular, since in Ireland an army representative of the people would be largely Catholic, and much former difficulty arose from Catholics in Ireland meeting with opposition from some Catholic authorities. It may be seen the position is delicate as well as difficult, and in writing a preliminary note one point should be emphasised. We must not evade a difficulty because it is delicate and dangerous, and we must not temporise. In a physical contest on the field of battle it is allowable to use tactics and strategy, to retreat as well as advance, to have recourse to a ruse as well as open attack; but *in matters of principle there can be no tactics, there is one straightforward course to follow, and that course must be found and followed without swerving to the end.*

CHAPTER XVII

RESISTANCE IN ARMS—THE TRUE MEANING OF LAW

I

WHEN we stand up to question false authority we should first make our footing firm by showing we understand true authority and uphold it. Let us be clear then as to the meaning of the word law. It may be defined; an ordinance of reason, the aim of which is the public good and promulgated by the ruling power. Let us cite a few authorities. "A human law bears the character of law so far as it is in conformity with right reason; and in that point of view it is manifestly derived from the Eternal Law." (*Aquinas Ethicus*, Vol. 1, p. 276.) Writing of laws that are unjust either in respect to end, author or form, St. Thomas says : " Such proceedings are rather acts of violence than laws; because St. Augustine says : 'A law that is not just goes for no law at all.'" (*Aquinas Ethicus*, Vol. 1, p. 292.) "The fundamental idea of all law," writes Balmez, "is that it be in accordance with reason, that it be an emanation from reason, an application of reason to society" (*European Civilisation*, Chap. 53). In the same chapter Balmez quotes St. Thomas with approval : " The kingdom is not made for the king, but the king for the kingdom"; and he goes on to the natural inference : "That all governments have been established for the good of society, and that this alone should be the compass to guide those who are in command, whatever be the form of government." It is likewise the view of Mill, in *Representative Government*, that the well-being of the governed is the sole object of government. It was the view of Plato before the Christian era : his ideal city should be established, "that the whole City might be in the happiest condition." (*The Republic*, Book 4.) Calderwood writes : " Political Government can be legitimately constructed only on condition of the acknowledgment of natural obligations and rights as inviolable." (*Handbook of Modern Philosophy, Applied Ethics*, Sec. 4.) Here all schools and all times are in agreement. Till these conditions are fulfilled for us we are at war. When an independent and genuine Irish Government is established we shall yield it a full and hearty allegiance : the law shall then be in repute. We do not stand now to deny the idea of authority, but to say that the wrong people are in authority, the wrong flag is over us.

II

"We must overthrow the arguments that might be employed against us by the advocates of blind submission to any power that happens to be established," writes Balmez, on resistance to *De Facto* Governments. (*European Civilisation*, Chap. 55.) We could not be more explicit than the famous Spanish theologian. To such arguments let the following stand out from his long and emphatic reply :—"Illegitimate authority is no authority at all; the idea of power involves the idea of right, without which it is mere physical power, that is force." He writes further : "The conqueror, who, by mere

force of arms, has subdued a nation, does
not thereby acquire a right to its posses-
sion; the government, which by gross
iniquities has despoiled entire classes of
citizens, exacted undue contributions,
abolished legitimate rights, cannot justify
its acts by the simple fact of its having sufficient strength to execute these
iniquities." There is much that is equally
clear and definite. What extravagant
things can be said on the other side by
people in high places we know too well.
Balmez in the same book and chapter gives
an excellent example and an excellent
reply : "Don Felix Amat, Archbishop of
Palmyra, in the posthumous work entitled
Idea of the Church Militant, makes use of
these words : 'Jesus Christ, by His plain
and expressive answer, *Render to Cæsar
the things that are Cæsar's*, has sufficiently
established that the mere fact of a government's existence is sufficient for enforcing
the obedience of subjects to it. . . .'
His work was forbidden at Rome," is
Balmez' expressive comment, and he continues, "and whatever may have been the
motives for such a prohibition, we may rest
assured that, in the case of a book advo-
cating such doctrines, every man who is

jealous of his rights might acquiesce in the decree of the Sacred Congregation." So much for *De Facto* Government. It is usurpation; by being consummated it does not become legitimate. When its decrees are not resisted, it does not mean we accept them in principle—nor can we even pretend to accept them—but that the hour to resist has not yet come. It is the strategy of war.

III

We stand on the ground that the English Government in Ireland is founded in usurpation and as such deny its authority. But if it be argued, assuming it as Ireland's case, that a usurped authority, gradually acquiesced in by the people, ultimately becomes the same as legitimate, the reply is still clear. For ourselves we meet the assumption with a simple denial, appealing to Irish History for evidence that we never acquiesced in the English Usurpation. But to those who are not satisfied with this simple denial, we can point out that even an authority, originally founded legitimately, may be resisted when abusing its power to the ruin of the Commonwealth. We still stand on the ground that the English government is founded in usurpation, but we can dispose of all objections by proving the extremer case. This is the case Dr. Murray, already quoted, discusses. " The question," he writes, " is about resistance to an established and legitimate government which abuses its power." (*Essays, Chiefly Theological,* Vol. 4.) He continues : " The common opinion of a large number of our theologians, then, is that it is lawful to resist by force, and if necessary to depose, the sovereign ruler or rulers, in the extreme— the very extreme—case wherein the following conditions are found united :

1. The tyranny must be excessive—intolerable.
2. The tyranny must be manifest, manifest to men of good sense and right feeling.
3. The evils inflicted by the tyrant must be greater than those which would ensue from resisting and deposing him.
4. There must be no other available way of getting rid of the tyranny except by recurring to the extreme course.
5. There must be a moral certainty of success.
6. The revolution must be one conducted

or approved by the community at large . . . the refusal of a small party in the State to join with the over-whelming mass of their countrymen would not render the resistance of the latter unlawful." (*Essays, Chiefly Theological;* see also Rickaby, *Moral Philosophy,* Chap. 8, Sec. 7.)

Some of these conditions are drawn out at much length by Dr. Murray. I give what is outstanding. How easily they could fit Irish conditions must strike any-one. I think it might fairly be said that our leaders generally would, if asked to lay down conditions for a rising, have framed some more stringent than these. It might be said, in truth, of some of them that they seem to wait for more than a moral cer-tainty of success, an absolute certainty, that can never be looked for in war.

IV

When a government through its own iniquity ceases to exist, we must, to estab-lish a new government on a true and just basis, go back to the origin of Civil Authority. No one argues now for the Divine Right of Kings, but in studying the

old controversy we get light on the subject
of government that is of all time. To the
conception that kings held their power
immediately from God, " Suarez boldly
opposed the thesis of the initial sovereignty
of the people; from whose consent, therefore, all civil authority immediately
sprang. So also, in opposition to Melanch-
thon's theory of governmental omni-
potence, Suarez *a fortiori* admitted the
right of the people to depose those princes
who would have shown themselves unworthy of the trust reposed in them." (De
Wulf, *History of Medieval Philosophy*,
Third Edition, p. 495.) Suarez' refutation
of the Anglican theory, described by
Hallam as clear, brief, and dispassionate,
has won general admiration. Hallam
quotes him to the discredit of the English
divines : " For this power, by its very
nature, belongs to no one man but
to a multitude of men. This is a
certain conclusion, being common to all
our authorities, as we find by St. Thomas,
by the Civil laws, and by the great
canonists and casuists; all of whom agree
that the prince has that power of law-
giving which the people have given him.
And the reason is evident, since all men

are born equal, and consequently no one
has a political jurisdiction over another,
nor any dominion; nor can we give any
reason from the nature of the thing why
one man should govern another rather
than the contrary." (Hallam—*Literature
of Europe*, Vol. 3, Chap. 4.) Dr. Murray,
in the essay already quoted, speaks of Sir
James Mackintosh as the ablest Protestant
writer who refuted the Anglican theory,
which Mackintosh speaks of as " The ex-
travagance of thus representing obedience
as the only duty without an exception."
Dr. Murray concludes his own essay on
Resistance to the Supreme Civil Power by
a long passage from Mackintosh, the
weight and wisdom of which he praises.
The greater part of the passage is devoted
to the difficulties even of success and em-
phasising the terrible evils of failure.   In
what has already been written here I have
been at pains rather to lay bare all possible
evils than to hide them.   But when revolt
has become necessary and inevitable, then
the conclusion of the passage Dr. Murray
quotes should be endorsed by all : " An insurrection rendered necessary by oppression, and warranted by a reasonable
probability of a happy termination, is an

act of public virtue, always environed with so much peril as to merit admiration." Yes, and given the happy termination, the right and responsibility of establishing a new government rest with the body of the people.

V

We come, then, to this conclusion, that government is just only when rightfully established and for the public good; that usurpation not only may but ought to be resisted; that an authority originally legitimate once it becomes habitually tyrannical may be resisted and deposed; and that when from abuse or tyranny a particular government ceases to exist, we have to re-establish a true one. It is sometimes carelessly said, "Liberty comes from anarchy," but this is a very dangerous doctrine. It would be nearer truth to say from anarchy inevitably comes tyranny. Men receive a despot to quell a mob. But when a people, determined and disciplined, resolve to have neither despotism nor anarchy but freedom, then they act in the light of the Natural Law. It is well put in the doctrine of St. Thomas, as given by Turner in his *History of Philosophy*

(Chap. 38) : " The redress to which the subjects of a tyrant have a just right must be sought, not by an individual, but by an authority temporarily constituted by the people and acting according to law." Yes, and when wild and foolish people talk hysterically of our defiance of all authority, let us calmly show we best understand the basis of Authority—which is Truth, and most highly reverence its presiding spirit—which is Liberty.

CHAPTER XVIII

RESISTANCE IN ARMS—OBJECTIONS

II

HAVING stated the case for resistance, it will serve us to consider some objections. Many inquiring minds may be made happy by a clear view of the doctrine, till some clever opponent holds them up with remarks on prudence, possibly sensible, or remarks on revolutionists, most probably wild, with, perhaps, the authority of a great name, or unfailing refuge in the concrete. It is curious that while often noticed how men, trying to evade a concrete issue, take refuge in the abstract, it is not noticed that men, trying to avoid acknowledging the truth of some principle, take refuge in the concrete. A living and pressing difficulty, though transient, looms larger than any historical fact or coming danger. Seeing this, we may restore confidence to a baffled mind, by helping it to distinguish the contingent from the permanent. Thus, by disposing of objections, we make our ground secure.

II

To the name of prudence the most imprudent people frequently appeal. Those whose one effort is to evade difficulties, who to cover their weakness plead patience, would be well advised to consider how men passionately in earnest, enraged by these evasions, pour their scorn on patience as a thing to shun. The plea does not succeed; it only for the moment damages the prestige of a great name. Patience is not a virtue of the weak but of the strong. An objector says : "Of course, all this is right in the abstract, but consider the frightful abuses in practice," and some apt replies spring to mind. Dr. Murray, writing on "Mental Reservation," in his *Essays, chiefly Theological*, speaks thus : "But it is no objection to any principle of morals to say that unscrupulous men will abuse it, or that, if publicly preached to such and

Q

such an audience or in such and such circumstances, it will lead to mischief." This
is admirable, to which the objector can
only give some helpless repetitions. With
Balmez, we reply : "But in recommending
prudence to the people let us not disguise
it under false doctrines—let us beware of
calming the exasperation of misfortune by
circulating errors subversive of all governments, of all society." (*European Civilisation*, Chap. 55.) Of men who shrink from
investigating such questions, Balmez
wrote : "I may be permitted to observe
that their prudence is quite thrown away,
that their foresight and precaution are of
no avail. Whether they investigate these
questions or not, they *are* investigated,
agitated and decided, in a manner that we
must deplore." (*Ibid.* Chap. 54.) Take
with this Turner on France under the old
régime and the many and serious griev-
ances of the people : "The Church, whose
duty it was to inculcate justice and forbearance, was identified, in the minds of
the people, with the Monarchy which they
feared and detested." (*History of Philosophy*, Chap. 59.) The moral is that when
injustice and evil are rampant, let us have
no palliation, no weakness disguising itself

as a virtue. What we cannot at once resist, we can always repudiate. To ignore these things is the worst form of imprudence—an imprudence which we, for our part at least, take the occasion here heartily to disclaim.

III

There is so much ill-considered use of the word revolutionist, we should bear in mind it is a strictly relative term. If the freedom of a people is overthrown by treachery and violence, and oppression practised on their once thriving land, that is a revolution, and a bad revolution. If, with tyranny enthroned and a land wasting under oppression, the people rise and by their native courage, resource and patience re-establish in their original independence a just government, that is a revolution, and a good revolution. The revolutionist is to be judged by his motives, methods and ends; and, when found true, his insurrection, in the words of Mackintosh, is " an act of public virtue." It is the restoration of Truth to its place of honour among men.

IV

Balmez mentions Bossuet as apparently
one who denies the right here maintained;
and we may with profit read some things
Bossuet has said in another context, yet
which touches closely what is our concern.
Writing of *Les Empires*, thus Bossuet:
"Les révolutions des empires sont réglées
par la providence, et servent à humilier les
princes." This is hardly calculated to de-
ter us from a bid for freedom; and if we go
on to read what he has written further
under this heading, we get testimony to the
hardihood and love of freedom and country
that distinguished early Greece and Rome
in language of eloquence that might in-
flame any people to liberty. Of undegenerate Greece, free and invincible:
"Mais ce que la Grece avait de plus grand
était une politique ferme et prévoyante,
qui savait abandonner, hasarder et dé-
fendre, ce qu'il fallait; et, ce qui est plus
grand encore, un courage que l'amour de
la liberté et celui de la patrie rendaient
invincible." Of undegenerate Rome, her
liberty: "La liberté leur était donc
un trésor qu'ils préferoient à toutes
les richesses de l'univers." Again: "La

maxime fondamentale de la république était de regarder la liberté comme une chose inséparable du nom Roman." And her constancy : " Voila de fruit glorieux de la patience Romaine. Des peuples qui s'enhardissaient et se fortifiaient par leurs malheurs avaient bien raison de croire qu'on sauvait tout pourvu qu'on ne perdit pas l'espérance." And again : " Parmi eux, dans les états les plus tristes, jamais les faibles conseils n'ont été seulement écoutés." The reading of such a fine tribute to the glory of ancient liberties is not likely to diminish our desire for freedom; rather, to add to the natural stimulus found in our own splendid traditions, the further stimulus of this thought that must whisper to us : " Persevere and conquer, and to-morrow our finest opponent will be our finest panegyrist when the battle has been fought and won."

v

In conclusion, in the concrete this simple fact will suffice : we have established immutable principles; the concrete circumstances are contingent and vary. It is admirably put in the following passage :

"The historical and sociological sciences, so carefully cultivated in modern times, have proved to evidence that social conditions *vary* with the epoch and the country, that they are the resultant of quite a number of fluctuating influences, and that, accordingly, the science of Natural Right should not merely establish *immutable* principles bearing on the moral end of man, but should likewise deal with the *contingent* circumstances accompanying the application of those principles." (De Wulf, *Scholasticism, Old and New*, Part 2, Chap. 2, Sec. 33.) Yes, and if we apply principles to-morrow, it is not with the conditions of to-day we must deal, but "with the contingent circumstances accompanying the application of those principles." Let that be emphasised. The conditions of twenty years ago are vastly changed to-day; and how altered the conditions of to-morrow can be, how astonishing can be the change in the short span of twenty years, let this fact prove. Ireland in '48 was prostrate after a successful starvation and an unsuccessful rising—to all appearances this time hopelessly crushed; yet within twenty years another rising was planned that shook English government in

Ireland to its foundations. Let us bear in mind this further from De Wulf : "Sociology, understood in the wider and larger sense, is transforming the methods of the science of Natural Right." In view of that transformation he is wise who looks to to-morrow. What De Wulf concludes we may well endorse, when he asks us to take facts as they are brought to light and study "each question on its merits, in the light of these facts and not merely in its present setting but as presented in the pages of history." It can be fairly said of those who have always stood for the separation of Ireland from the British Empire, that they alone have always appealed to historical evidence, have always regarded the conditions of the moment as transient, have always discussed possible future contingencies. The men who temporised were always hypnotised by the conditions of the hour. But in the life-story of a nation stretching over thousands of years, the British occupation is a contingent circumstance, and the immutable principle is the Liberty of the Irish People.

CHAPTER XIX

THE BEARNA BAOGHAIL—CONCLUSION

I

B UT when principles have been proved and objections answered, there are still some last words to say for some who stand apart—the men who held the breach. For, they do stand apart, not in error but in constancy; not in doubt of the truth but its incarnation; not average men of the multitude for whom human laws are made, who must have moral certainty of success, who must have the immediate allegiance of the people. For it is the distinguishing glory of our prophets and our soldiers of the forlorn hope, that the defeats of common men were for them but incentives to further battle; and when they held out against the prejudices of their time, they were not standing in some new conceit, but most often by prophetic insight fighting for a forgotten truth of yesterday, catching in their souls to light them forward, the hidden glory of to-morrow. They knew to be theirs by anticipation the general allegiance without which lesser men cannot proceed. They knew they stood for the Truth, against which nothing can prevail, and if they had to endure struggle, suffering and pain, they had the finer knowledge born of these things, a knowledge to which the best of men ever win—that if it is a good thing to live, it is a good thing also to die. Not that they despised life or lightly threw it away; for none better than they knew its grandeur, none more than they gloried in its beauty, none were so happily full as they of its music; but they knew, too, the value of this deep truth, with the final loss of which Earth must perish : the man who is afraid to die is not fit to live. And the knowledge for them stamped out Earth's oldest fear, winning for life its highest ecstasy. Yes, and when one or more of them had to stand in the darkest generation and endure all penalties to the extreme penalty, they knew for all that they had had the best of life and did not

count it a terrible thing if called by a little
to anticipate death. They had still the
finest appreciation of the finer attributes
of comradeship and love; but it is part of
the mystery of their happiness and success,
that they were ready to go on to the end,
not looking for the suffrage of the living
nor the monuments of the dead. Yes, and
when finally the re-awakened people by
their better instincts, their discipline, patriotism and fervour, will have massed into
armies, and marched to freedom, they will
know in the greatest hour of triumph that
the success of their conquering arms was
made possible by those who held the
breach.

II

When, happily, we can fall back on the
eloquence of the world's greatest orator,
we turn with gratitude to the greatest tribute ever spoken to the memory of those
men to whom the world owes most.
Demosthenes, in the finest height of his
finest oration, vindicates the men of every
age and nation who fight the forlorn hope.
He was arraigned by his rival, Æschines,
for having counselled the Athenians to
pursue a course that ended in defeat, and

he replies thus : " If, then, the results had
been foreknown to all—not even then
should the Commonwealth have abandoned her design, if she had any regard for
glory, or ancestry, or futurity. As it is, she
appears to have failed in her enterprise, a
thing to which all mankind are liable, if
the Deity so wills it." And he asks the
Athenians : " Why, had we resigned without a struggle that which our ancestors
encountered every danger to win, who
would not have spit upon you ?" And he
asks them further to consider strangers,
visiting their City, sunk in such degradation, " especially when in former times our
country had never preferred an igno-
minious security to the battle for honour."
And he rises from the thought to this
proud boast : " None could at any period of
time persuade the Commonwealth to
attach herself in secure subjection to the
powerful and unjust; through every age
has she persevered in a perilous struggle
for precedency and honour and glory."
And he tells them, appealing to the
memory of Themistocles, how they
honoured most their ancestors who acted
in such a spirit : " Yes; the Athenians of
that day looked not for an orator or a

general, who might help them to a pleasant servitude,: they scorned to live if it could not be with freedom.". And he pays them, his listeners, a tribute : " What I declare is, that such principles are your own; I show that before my time such was the spirit of the Commonwealth." From one eloquent height to another he proceeds, till, challenging Æschines for arraigning him, thus counselling the people, he rises to this great level : " But, never, never can you have done wrong, O Athenians, in undertaking the battle for the freedom and safety of all : I swear it by your forefathers—those that met the peril at Marathon, those that took the field at Platæa, those in the sea-fight at Salamis, and those at Artimesium, and many other brave men who repose in the public monuments, all of whom alike, as being worthy of the same honour, the country buried, Æschines, not only the successful and victorious." We did not need this fine eloquence to assure us of the greatness of our O'Neills and our Tones, our O'Donnells and our Mitchels, but it so quickens the spirit and warms the blood to read it, it so touches—by the admiration won from ancient and modern times—an enduring principle of the human heart—

the capacity to appreciate a great deed and rise over every physical defeat—that we know in the persistence of the spirit we shall come to a veritable triumph. Yes; and in such light we turn to read what Ruskin called the greatest inscription ever written, that which Herodotus tells us was raised over the Spartans, who fell at Thermopylæ, and which Mitchel's biographer quotes as most fitting to epitomise Mitchel's life : "Stranger, tell thou the Lacedemonians that we are lying here, having obeyed their words." And the biographer of Mitchel is right in holding that he who reads into the significance of these brave lines, reads a message not of defeat but of victory.

III

Yes; and in paying a fitting tribute to those great men who are our exemplars, it would be fitting also, in conclusion, to remember ourselves as the inheritors of a great tradition; and it would well become us not only to show the splendour of the banner that is handed on to us, but to show that this banner *we*, too, are worthy to bear. For, how often it shall be victorious and how high it shall be planted, will depend on the conception we have of its supreme greatness, the knowledge that it can be fought for in all times and places, the conviction that we may, when least we expect, be challenged to deny it; and that by our bearing we may bring it new credit and glory or drag it low in repute. We do well, I say, to remember these things. For in our time it has grown the fashion to praise the men of former times but to deny their ideal of Independence; and we who live in that ideal, and in it breathe the old spirit, and preach it and fight for it and prophesy for it an ultimate and complete victory—we are young men, foolish and unpractical. And what should be our reply? A reply in keeping with the flag, its history and its destiny. Let them, who deride or pity us, see we despise or pity their standards, and let them know by our works—lest by our election they misunderstand—that we are not without ability in a freer time to contest with them the highest places—avoiding the boast, not for an affected sense of modesty but for a saving sense of humour. For in all the vanities of this time that make Life and Literature choke with absurdities, pretensions and humbug, let us have no new

folly. Let us with the old high confidence
blend the old high courtesy of the
Gaedheal. Let us grow big with our cause.
Shall we honour the flag we bear by a
mean, apologetic front? No! Wherever it
is down, lift it; wherever it is challenged,
wave it; wherever it is high, salute it;
wherever it is victorious, glorify and exult
in it. At all times and forever be for it
proud, passionate, persistent, jubilant, de-
fiant; stirring hidden memories, kindling
old fires, wakening the finer instincts of
men, till all are one in the old spirit, the
spirit that will not admit defeat, that has
been voiced by thousands, that is noblest
in Emmet's one line, setting the time for
his epitaph : " *When* my country "—not *if*
—but "*when* my country takes her place
among the nations of the earth." It is no
hypothesis; it is a certainty. There have
been in every generation, and are in our
own, men dull of apprehension and cold of
heart, who could not believe this, but we
believe it, we live in it : *we know it.* Yes,
we know it, as Emmet knew it, and as it
shall be seen to-morrow; and when the
historian of to-morrow, seeing it accomplished, will write its history, he will not
note the end with surprise. Rather will he

marvel at the soul in constancy, rivalling the best traditions of undegenerate Greece and Rome, holding through disasters, persecutions, suffering, and not less through the seductions of milder but meaner times, seeing through all shining clearly the goal : he will record it all, and, still marvelling, come to the issue that dauntless spirit has reached, proud and happy; but he will write of that issue—*Liberty; Inevitable* : in two words to epitomise the history of a people that is without a parallel in the Annals of the World.

THE END

L5